No. 625

CATALOGUE
OF
IMPORTANT BOOKS
ON
ROMAN AND ANCIENT FOREIGN LAW

SPRINGER-SCIENCE+BUSINESS MEDIA, B.V.

Cable address: Books Hague. Teleph. 111017

Prices are in Dutch guilders

1 guilder is about $ 0.55 = £ 0.2.3.

My american customers may send their orders through Messrs TICE & LYNCH, forwarding agents, 21 Pearl Street, New York City.

ISBN 978-94-015-1543-6 ISBN 978-94-015-2657-9 (eBook)
DOI 10.1007/978-94-015-2657-9
Softcover reprint of the hardcover 1st edition 1939

ROMAN AND ANCIENT FOREIGN LAW

1 **Albrecht, W. E.,** Die Gewere als Grundlage des ältern deutschen Sachenrechts. Königsberg, 1828. bound. 6.—
2 **Aller, K. van,** Generaale regulen, en definitien van beschreeve Romeynsche rechten, mitsg. verhandel. van de pynbank. 2e verb. dr. Dordrecht, J. 't Hooft, 1729. 4to. vellum. 4.50
3 — — The same. 3e dr. Dordr., J. G. Wittich, 1761. 4to. 5.50
4 **Alonso, J.,** Recopilacion y comentarios de los fueros y leyes del antiguo reino de Navarra. Madrid, 1848, 49. 2 vols. in 1. Hfcalf. 20.—
5 **Altamiranus, H.,** De filiis official. militar. qui in bello moriuntur. Matrit. 1648. W. front. fol. limp vellum. 6.—
6 **Althusius, J.,** Dicaelogicae ll. III, totum jus, quo utimur, methodicè complectentes, cum parallelis hujus et Judaici juris. Herbornae, 1617. 4to. vellum. 90.—

Extremely scarce first edition of this complete system of Roman law, distinguishing itself from contemporary works by its concise dialectic form.

The titlepage bears 2 stamps and inscriptions in old ms. As usual paperspotted.

7 **Anania, J. de,** Super primo decretalium. In primum decretalium lectura dilucida. Super secundo el tertio decretalium super quinto decretalium. Additionibus Andr. Barbatiae. Lugduni, P. Fradin, 1550, 1553. 2 vols. folio. oaken boards, back pressed pigskin. (Some small wormholes but a clean copy). 20.—

The index is defective (B 4, 5 and E. 3–6 are lacking).

8 **Andreae, J. H.,** De Francisco Fabricio Marcodurano. Heidelb. 1763. 4to. 1.—
9 **Annalen** der Gesetzgebung und Rechtsgelehrsamkeit in den Preussischen Staaten hrsg. von E. F. Klein. Berlin, 1788. 2 vols. Hfcalf. 5.—
10 **Annotations,** consultations et avis sur le droit coutumier, émanés des avocats les plus distingués au Conseil du Flandre et au grand Conseil de Malines, aux 17e et 18e siècles. (Publ. par Ph. van de Velde). Gand, 1852. Hfcloth. 5.—
11 **Anquetil Duperron,** Législation orientale, montrant quels sont en Turquie, en Perse et dans l'Indoustan les principes fondamentaux du gouvernement. Amst., M. M. Rey, 1778. 4to. Hfmor. 17.50
12 **Anselmo, A.,** Consultat. seu resolut. et advisamenta diurna, d.i. Dagelijcxse consultatien, resolutien, enz. (in latin or in dutch). Antv. 1671. fol. calf. 7.50
13 **Antonellus, J. C.,** De tempore legali. Ven. 1670. fol. vellum.
14 — The same. Ven. 1692. fol. vellum. 5.—
15 **Antoninus, M.,** Variae resolut. in foro ecclesiast. civili etc. Papiae, 1606. fol. vellum. 7.—
16 **Archives** d'histoire du droit oriental. Publ. sous la dir. de J. Pirenne avec la collab. de A. Christensen, P. Collinet, H. Duesberg, B. Hrozný, J. H. Kramers, A. Soloviev e.a. Brux. 1937. Vol. I. 18.50

This vol. contains: Orient ancien — Orient gréco-romain — Orient médiéval.

17 **d'Argentré, B.,** Commentarii in patrias Britonum leges, seu consuetudines generales antiquiss. ducatus Britanniae. Ed. 7a. Paris, 1661. fol. calf. 25.—
18 **d'Arnaud, G.,** Variar. coniect. Franeker, M. van der Veen, 1738. 4to. calf. 7.50
19 **Arrest** du Conseil privé du Roy, portant descharge au profit des marchands trafiquans sur la rivière de Loire de l'impost et contribution que les échevins de Nevers avaient obtenue.... pour lever certains droits sur lesmarchandises de bois et vins passans sur la dite rivière. Orleans, 1631. — **Arrest** etc. sur la demande intentée par les marchands frequentans la rivière, contre les maire et eschevins d'Angers pour raison des 300 livres de pention à eux deuë. Orleans, 1643. — Tog. 2 pieces. sm. 8vo. 7.50
20 **Asinus, J. B.,** Commentarii in titulum digestorum de religiosis et sumptibus funerum. Florentia, L. Torrentinus, 1562. folio. calf. (Binding rubbed, otherwise a fine copy). 15.—
21 **Assises** de Jérusalem ou recueil des ouvrages de jurisprudence composés pendant le 13e siècle dans les Royaumes de Jérusalem et de Chypre. Publié p. Beugnot. Paris, 1841, 43. 2 vols. large folio. Hfcalf. 150.—

Published in the Recueil des historiens des croisades.
Very scarce.

22 **Auto** do iuramenta que el rey Philippe II fez aos tres estados deste Reyno, et do que elles fizerão a sua Mag., do reconhecimento, et aceitação do Principe dom Phelippe, nosso senhor, seu filho. Em Lisboa à 14 Julho de 1619. Lisboa, 1619. — **Allegaçoes** que fes Fr. Leitão pera informacão de sua iustica na causa em que o accusa Fr. Vaz de Gouvea. Lisboa, 1618. — **Gouvea,** Allegaçan, na qual se mostra por dirito, por breues dos sũmos Põtifices, por Aluaràs dos senhores Reys, por sentenças em juizo contencioso, por consultas da mesa da consciencia etc. — Tog. 12 pieces in 1 vol. sm. fol. calf. 48.—

23 **Automne, B.,** La conférence du droict français avec le droict romain. 2e éd' Paris, 1615· 4to. calf. 8.50

24 **Aymus, B.,** De universo alluvionum jure (von Zuwachs- oder Auflösungs-Recht). Ed. c. not. stud. A. Fritschi. Jenae, 1675. W. 3 pl. and woodcuts in the text. 4to. 4.50

25 **Bacquet, J.,** Oeuvres. Augm. de plusieurs questions, decisions et arrests des cours de France par C. de Ferrière. Paris, 1688. fol. calf. 25.—

26 **Baitellus, P.,** De ultimis voluntatibus decisiones. Genevae, 1687. fol. vellum. 6.—

27 **Baldasseroni, A.,** Leggi e costumi del cambio. Ed. 2a. Firenze, 1796. fol. Hfvellum. 3.50

28 **Balduinus, F.,** Ad leges de jure civili, Voconiam, Falcidiam, Juliam Papiam Poppaeam, Rhodiam, Aquiliam. Acc. de jure civili ex Papiniano, etc. Halae, 1730. vellum. 3.50

29 **Bally, G.,** Traité des laods et trezeins. 2e éd., des servis, et des taillables. Av. édit sur la valeur des espèces. Anneci, (ab. 1745). sm. 8vo. vellum. 5.—

30 **Balmaseda, D.,** De collectis et tributis praesertim in Hispania indictis. Ed. Gallica auct. expurg. Lugd. 1725. fol. Hfvellum. 5.—

31 **Bar, L. von,** Das Beweisurtheil des germanischen Processes. Hannover, 1866. Bound. 2.—

32 **Bargalius, C.,** De dolo. Hanov. 1604. fol. vellum. 6.—

33 **Baronius, F.,** De effect. minoris, aetatis circa contractus, ultimas voluntates etc. Panormi, 1661. fol. Hfvellum. 5.—

34 **Bartholomaeus a Saliceto,** Opera omnia. Francof. 1615. 6 vols. in 2. folio. Half stamped pigskin. 200.—

[Commentarii] in Codicis libros. 4 vols. — Pars unica in secundam Digesti veteris partem. — Repertorium.

35 — In Codicis libros commentaria. Venetiis, 1586. With Repertorium. 4 vols. in 3. folio. vellum. 40.—

Vol. II is lacking. A few leaves of vol. IV discoloured.

36 **Bartolus a Saxoferrato,** Opera omnia. Venetiis, 1585. 12 vols. in 10. fol. vellum. 250.—

A few vols. slightly waterstained, the margins of one vol. repaired, another vol. a little wormed, but alltogether a very sound copy.

37 — **Kamp, J. L. J. van de,** Bartolus de Saxoferrato 1313–1357. Leven, werken, invloed, beteekenis. Amst. 1936. 4.50

38 **Bartsch, R.,** Die Rechtsstellung der Frau als Gattin und Mutter. Geschichtl. Entwicklung ihrer persönlichen Stellung im Privatrecht bis in das 17. Jahrh. Lpz. 1903. 2.50

39 **Bauer, O.,** Die Dareingabe beim Kauf nach römischem Rechte. München, 1887. 1.—

40 **Bayer, A.,** Alt-Ansbacher Recht in neuer Zeit. Ansbach, 1908. 1.—

41 **Beccaria, C.,** Opere. C. discorsa sulla vita e le opere dell' autore di P. Villari. Firenze, 1854. 1.50

42 **(—)** Traité des délits et des peines. Trad. de l' ital..... avec des addit. de l'auteur, qui n'ont pas encore paru en ital. (par Morellet). Lausanne, 1766. sm. 8vo. calf, gilt back. 18.—

43 **Beck, J. A.,** Vollständiges Wechsel-Recht. Nürnberg, 1751. W. front. 4to. calf. 24.—

44 **Behamb, J. F.,** I. Neu revid. und mit 117 decid. Casibus, verm. Rosz-Tauscher-Recht. Nebst Anh. aus J. W. Rövenstrunck Meditat. aedilit. II. Das Rosz-Ausleiher-Recht. III. Salander, Fuhr-Manns-Recht. Francof. 1715. 4to. 4.50

45 **Bekker, E. I.,** Die Aktionen des Röm. Privatrechts. Berlin, 1871, 73. 2 vols. in 1. bound. 5.—

46 **Bellonus, A.,** De iure accressendi. Ven. 1672. 3 vols. fol. vellum. (Titlepage of the second vol. is missing). 5.—

47 **Below, G. von,** Territorium und Stadt. Aufsätze zur deutschen Verfassungs-, Verwaltungs- u. Wirtschaftsgesch. 1900. 4.—

48 — Der deutsche Staat des Mittelalters. Grundriss der deutschen Verfassungsgeschichte. Lpz. 1914. 4.—

49 **Benedictus XIV,** De synodo dioecesana. Bassani, 1767. 2 vols. in 1. W. portrait. fol. vellum. 4.50

50 **Bergwerks-Ordnung.** Vermehret mit einer.2en Verzeichnusz sowohl der Artikeln, als deren Inhalts. Grätz, ab. 1700. sm. fol. Hfcalf. 9.—

51 **Bersanus, B.,** De viduis. Genevae, 1699. fol. limp vellum. 7.50

52 — De pupillis, eorum privillegiis et iuribus. Lugd. 1705. fol. vellum. 6.—

53 **Bethmann-Hollweg, M. A. von,** Ursprung der Lombard. Städtefreiheit. Bonn, 1846. Bound. 3.50

54 **Beust, J. E. von,** Sciagraphia juris monetandi in sacro imperio Romano-Germanico. Oder Entwurf von der Münzgerechtigkeit im Heil. Römisch-Teutschen Reich. Lpz. 1745. 4to. calf. 12.—,

55 **Bibliothèque d'histoire du droit normand.** 1re Série: Textes. 2e Série: Etudes. Caen 1910–31. 1st Series, vol. I–VI; 2d series, vol. I–IV. Tog. 10 vols. 50.—

Contains: **Arresta communia scacarii.** (1276–1290. 1291–1294). Publ. par E. Perrot. — **Instructions** et ensaignemens .Style de procéder d'une justice seigneuriale normande (1386–90). Par G. Besnier et R. Génestal. — **Mémorial** de l'échiquier des archevêques de Rouen, 5 juin 1381. Av. notes et introd. par F. Soudet. — **H. Pissard,** La clameur de Haro dans le droit normand.

56 **Biener, Chr. G.,** Diplomatische Untersuchung über die Rechte der Todttheilung in Baiern. Lpz. 1778. 4to. boards. 2.50

57 **Binding, K.,** Die Normen und ihre Uebertretung. Lpz. 1872, 77. 2 vols. in 1. Bound. 6.—

58 — — The same. 2e Aufl. Lpz. 1890–1919. 4 vols. in 5. Bound. 45.—

59 **Birnbaum, J. M. F.,** Die rechtliche Natur der Zehnten aus den Grundeigenthumsverhältnissen des römischen und fränkischen Reichs historisch entwickelt. Bonn, 1831 boards. 2.5.

60 **Bitsch, C.,** Tractatus de thesauris. Norib. 1674. sm. 8vo. vellum. 2.50

61 **Blätter, Zerstreute,** a. d. Hand- und Hülfsakten eines Juristes. Wissenschaftl. und Ge0 schichtl. a. d. Theorie und Praxis oder a. d. Lehre u. d. Leben des Rechts. Hrsg. von- K. F. Göschel. Erfurt, 1732–42. 3 vols. in 4. boards. 7.50

62 **Blumlacher, C.,** Commentarius in die peinliche Haslgerichts-Ordnung. 3er Dr. Salzburg, 1694. 4to. vellum. 3.—

63 **Bluntschli, J. C.,** Geschichte des allgemeinen Staatsrechts und der Politik. München, 1864. Bound. 9.—

Original imprint.

64 **Bodin, J.,** Les six livres de la République. Paris, 1577. fol. calf. 75.—

2d edition. Good copy. The upper margin of the titlepage missing, without loss of text.

65 — De republica ll. VI lat. ab auctore redditi. Ed. 3a. .... Multo emendatior. Francof., J. Wechel, 1594. 8vo.vellum. 60.—

66 — **Baudrillart, H.,** J. Bodin et son temps. Tableau des théories politiques, et des idées économiques au 16e siècle. Paris, 1853. Hfcalf. (Slightly paperspotted). 40.—

Very scarce and much sought after.

67 **Boehmer, G. P.,** Principia juris feudalis praes. Longobardici quod per Germaniam obtinet. Ed. 3a. Goett. 1775. boards. 3.50

68 **Böhmer, J. H.,** Jus ecclesiast. protestant. 3a–4a ed. Halae, 1730–40. 5 vols. W. portrait. 4to.vellum. 12.—

69 **Boerius, N.,** Decisiones supremi senatus Burdagalensis. Francof. 1665. fol. vellum. 10.—

70 **Bondenus, V.,** Notae, etc. ad tractatum de pascuis et iure pascendi Ant. Fernandez de Otero. Parmae, 1698. fol. vellum. 4.50

71 **Bonfinius, F. A.,** Decisiones florentiae. Pisae, 1760. fol. vellum. 3.75

72 **Bonjean, L. B.,** Traité des actions ou exposition histor. de l'organisation judiciaire et de la procédure civile chez les Romains. 2e éd. Paris, 1845. 2 vols. Hfcalf. 6.50

73 **Borgia, H.,** Investigat. iuris civilis. Neap. 1678. 2 vols. in 1. fol. vellum. 6.—

74 **Bornier, Ph.,** Conférences des nouvelles ordonnances de Louis XIV avec celles des rois prédecesseurs de Sa Majesté, le droit écrit, et les arrêts. Nouv. éd. Paris, 1700. 2 vols. 4to. calf. 5.—

75 — Conferences des ordonnances de Louis XIV, avec les anciennes ordonnances du royaume. Nouv. éd. Paris, 1737. 2 vols. 4to. calf. 7.50

76 **(Bosquet),** Dictionnaire raisonné des domaines et droits domaniaux. 2e éd. Rennes, 1782–84. 4 vols. in 2. 4to. calf. 12.—

Best edition.

77 **Bossius, J. A.,** De peculiari effectu contractus matrimonii nempe de dote filiabus danda. Lugd. 1662. fol. vellum. 3.50
78 — — The same. Flor. 1839. fol. Hfvellum. 2.—
79 — De effectu contractus matrimonii nempe de patria potestate in filios. Lugd. 1667. fol. vellum. 3.50
80 — — The same. Ed. 2a. Lugd. 1676, 94. 2 vols. in 1. fol. vellum. 6.—
81 **Bouché-Leclercq, A.,** Manuel des institutions Romaines. Paris, 1886. Hfcalf. 12.50
Out of print.
82 **Boucher,** Institutions commerciales, traitant de la jurisprudence marchande et des usages du négoce, d'après les anciennes et nouvelles lois; suivi d'un état de population de tous les royaumes, républiques, etc. et d'un projet de code de commerce. Paris, 1801. 4to. calf. 12.—
83 **Boucher d'Argis, A. G.,** Traité des gains nuptiaux et de survie qui sont en usage dans les pais de droit écrit. Lyon, 1738. 4to. calf. 5.—
84 **Boulversement** de la justice en 1771. Conten. le récit de ce qui s'est passé au parlement de Paris, les parlements de province, maximes du droit public françois etc. Et pièces y servant de suite. *Sous ce titre en ms. sont réunies 83 pièces,* dont quelques-unes en ms. Rel.-en 9 vol. Av. pl. d. veau. 15.—
Contient e.a.: Maximes du droit public français. 2 vol. (Red. p. Cl. Mey). — Maupeouana, ou correspondance du chancelier Maupeou avec son coeur Sorhouet. 2 vol. — Le parlement justifié par l'Impératrice de Russie. — Arrêtés, lois et édits du parlement.
85 **Boutaric, E.,** Saint Louis et Alfonse de Poitiers. Etude sur la réunion des provinces du Midi et de l'ouest à la couronne et sur les origines de la contradiction administrateur d'après les documents inédits. Paris, 1870. Hfmor., uncut. 7.50
86 — Explication de l'ordonnance de Louis XV, concernant les donations. Avignon, 1744. 4to. calf. 6.—
87 — Traité des droits seigneuriaux et des matières féodales. Nouv. éd. Toulouse, 1751. 4to. veau. 4.50
88 — Traité des matières beneficiales, contenant l'explication du Concordat et les institutions du droit canonique. (Toulouse), 1762. In 1 vol. 4to. calf. 5.—
89 **Braschius, M.,** De pleno arbitrio voluntatis in ultimis disposit. Ed. J. B. Braschius. Roma, 1722. fol. vellum. 3.50
90 **Bresslau, H.,** Handbuch der Urkundenlehre für Deutschland und Italien. Lpz. 1889. bound. (992 pp.). 6.—
91 **Bretonnier,** Recueil par ordre alphabétique des principales questions de droit qui se jugent diversement dans les différens tribunaux. 4e éd. Paris, 1769. 2 vols. sm. 8vo. calf. 4.50
92 **Brissonius, B.,** Selectarum ex jure civili antiquitatum ll. IIII. Ad legem Juliam de adulterijs, de solutionibus, de ritu nuptiarum, de jure conubiorum. Francof. 1587. fol. vellum. 20.—
Bound up with: **Hotoman, F.,** De verbis feudalibus, de legibus romanis, etc. Francof. 1587. — **Consuetudines** civitatum, et provinciarum Galliae. (Coutumes de Bourges, Orleans, Tours). Recogn. a D. Gothofredo. Francof. 1598.
93 — De verborum quae ad jus civile pertinent significatione. Cur. J. G. Heineccius. C. praef. J. H. Böhmeri. Ed. nova. Halae, 1743. W. front. fol. vellum. 10.—
94 **Bronchorst, E.,** Enantiophanon centuriae VI et conciliationes eorundem. Acc. de privilegiis studiosorum. Lugd. Bat., J. Marcus, 1621. 2 vols. in 1. 4to. vellum. 6.—
95 **Bruchstücke** aus den Schriften der Römischen Juristen. Gesamm. von H. E. Dirksen. Königsberg, 1814. sm. 8vo. 2.—
96 **Brunel de Granmaison, P.,** Dictionnaire des aydes, ou les dispositions der ordonnances de 1680 et 1681, etc. Nouv. éd. Paris, 1730. 2 vols. in 1. sm. 8vo. calf. 4.—
97 **Brunner, H.,** Zur Rechtsgeschichte der römischen und german. Urkunde. Berlin, 1880. Vol. I (all published). Bound. *Out of print and scarce.* 25.—
98 — Deutsche Rechtsgeschichte. 2e Aufl. Lpz. 1906. Vol. I. (Binding; Handb. II, 1). 7.50
99 **(Buddenbrock, G. J. von),** Sammlung der Gesetze, welche das heutige livländische Landrecht enthalten, kritisch bearb. Mitau, Riga, 1802–21. 2 vols. in 4. W. front.. 4to. Hfcalf. *Scarce.* 50.—
I. Angestammte livländische Landes-Rechte. — II, 1. Aeltere hinzugekommene Landesrechte. Landesordnungen, 1621–1710. 2 vols. — II. 2. und Anhang. Kirchenrecht und Richterregeln.

Prices are in Dutch guilders

100 **Bugnyon, Ph.,** Legum abrogatorum et inusitatarum in omnibus curiis, terris, jurisdictionibus regni Francicae tractatus. (In french). Ed. 2a. C. addit. etc. ed. L. F. Christyn. Brux. 1666. 4to. vellum. 9.—

101 **Bülow, F. von,** und **Th. Hagemann,** Practische Erörtungen aus allen Theilen der Rechts gelehrsamkeit, mit Urtheils-Sprüchen des Zelleschen Tribunals und der übr. Justizhöfe. Fortges. von E. Spangenberg. Hannover, 1798–1829. Vol. 1–8. 8 vols. 4to. boards. 3.50

102 **Bunge, F. G.,** Das liv- und esthländische Privatrecht. Tl. II. Das Familien- und Erbrecht. Dorpat, 1839. Bound. 2.25

103 **Burgundus, N.,** Ad consuetudines Flandriae aliarumque gentium tractatus controversiarum. Arnhem, 1670. sm. 8vo. vellum. 6.—

104 **Burman, L.,** De iure aureorum annulorum. Vom Recht der güldenen Ringe. Lps. 1740. 4to. 1.50

105 **Bynkershoek, C. van,** [Opera]. Lugd. Bat. 1710–44. 6 vols. 4to. calf. 40.—

Observatt. jur. Rom. 2 vol. — Opuscula. — Opera minora. — Quaest. jur. priv. — Quaest. jur. publ.

Large paper copy.

106 — Opera omnia. Lugd. Bat., S. et J. Luchtmans, 1767. 2 vols. in 1. With fine portrait by Houbraken. folio. Hfcalf. 36.—

107 — — The same. folio. 60.—

Very fine copy in old vellum gilt.

108 — Quaestiones iuris publici. 1° de rebus bellicis. 2° de rebus varii argumenti. Lugd. Bat., J. vanKerckhem, 1737. 4to. vellum. (At the beginning an insignificant wormhole). 10.—

109 — — Same work. Oxford, 1930. 2 vols. cloth. (The Classics of internat. law ed. by J. Brown Scott). 10.—

I. A photographic reproduction of the edition of 1737, with a list of errata, and portrait of B. — II. Translation of the text, with an introduction by J. de Louter, and indexes.

110 — Opuscula varii argumenti. Lugd. Bat., J. van der Linden, 1719. 4to. Hfcalf. 6.—

111 — Opera minora. Ed. 2a. Lugd. Bat., J. van Kerckhem, 1744. 4to. Hfcalf. 7.50

112 — Observationes tumultuariae. Ed. E. M. Meijers. A. S. de Blécourt et H. D. J. Bodenstein. The Hague, 1925, 34. Vol. I–II. 2 vols. roy. 8vo. buckram. 100.—

The ms. of the „Observationes tumultuariae'', long known to exist, but hitherto withheld from publication and lost sight of for more than a century, has been discovered. It consists of a complete set of reports of cases, decided by the Supreme Court of Holland, Zeeland and West Friesland during the very interesting period of 1704–1787, none of which has ever been published before. Van Bynkershoek was for 40 years a member of this Court and, during the latter part of the period, its president. His ms. was completed by his son-in-law W. Pauw, also a member of the Supreme Court and eventually its president, who added 10 vols. of „Observationes tumultuariae novae'' to the 14 vols. of van Bynkershoek. It is a monumental work and a most valuable contribution to the literature of international jurisprudences.

The „Observationes tumultuariae'' of van Bynkershoek will consist of 3 vols. of about 700 to 800 pp. each and will contain about 3000 judgments.

113 **Caballus, P.,** Resolut. criminales. Flor. 1606. fol. vellum. (back damaged). 3.50

114 **(Cabanel, de),** Maximes générales sur les droits domaniaux et seigneuriaux, tels que les lods et ventes, échanges, etc. 2e éd. Paris, 1755. sm. 8vo. calf. 4.—

115 **Cabrunus, A.,** De dote. Parmae, 1740. fol. boards. 3.50

116 **Caepolla, B.,** Varii tractatus. Lugd. 1547. vellum. 5.—

De servitutibus. Tractatus cautelarum, etc.

Titlepage and first leaf repaired.

117 **Caillet, J.,** De l'administration en France sous le ministère de Richelieu. 2me éd. Paris, 1861. 2 vols. in 1. Hfcalf. 2.—

118 **Calà, H.,** De restitutione in integrum. Neap. 1673. fol. vellum. 5.—

119 — De praeeminentia magnae curiae vicariae regni Neapolis. Neap. 1680. fol. vellum. 5.—

120 **Canisius, H.,** Opera de jure canonico. Lovan. 1649. 4to. vellum. 15.—

121 **Cannaert, J. B.,** Bijdr. tot het oude strafregt in België. 2e dr. Brussel, 1829. W. 2 lithogr. pl. 2.50

122 **Capdevila, A.,** Dharma, influencia del Oriente en el derecho de Roma. Cordoba, 1914. 7.50

Out of print.

123 **Caponus, Jul.,** Disceptationes forenses, ecclesiasticae, civiles et morales. Ven. 1705. 2 vols. in 1. fol. vellum. 4.50

124 **Carlevalius, T.,** Disputat. iuris variae. De iudiciis. Ven. 1660. 2 vols. in 1. fol. vellum. 4.50

125 — — The same. Ven. 1683. 2 vols. in 1. fol. vellum. 7.50

126 **Carocius, V.,** De deposito, oblationibus et sequestro. Ven., D. Zenarius, 1593. 4to. vellum. 5.—

127 **Casaregis, J. L. M.,** Discursus legales de commercio, in quibus assecurationes, naves, praedas, accomendas, etc. Tractatus de avariis G. Weytsen. 2a ed. Ven. 1740. 3 vols. folio. vellum. 60.—

128 **Cavalcanus, H.,** Practica et theorica de testibus. Ed. 3a. Marpurg, 1619. 4to. vellum. 4.50

129 **Cencius, P.,** De censibus, c. decisionibus Sacrae rotae Rom. Ven. 1621. 2 vols. in 1. fol. limp vellum. 3.—

130 — — The same. Ed. 2a adaucta comment. J. B. Leonellii ac L. Molinae. Aug. Taurin. 1621. fol. vellum. 5.—

131 — Additiones ad tractatum de censibus. Ven. 1629. fol. vellum. 4.—

132 **Chailland,** Dictionnaire raisonné des eaux et forêts. Paris, 1769. 2 vols. 4to. calf. 8.—

133 **Chesius, B.,** Interpretat. iuris. Ed. 2a. Liburni, 1657. 2 vols. in 1. fol. vellum. 5.—

134 **Christyn, J. B.,** Brabandts recht, d.i. generale costumen van Brabandt, Limborgh, Mechelen.... Bruss. 1682. 2 vols. calf. 30.—

135 **Civil-Prozeszordnung, Hessen-Darmstädtische,** von 1724 und peinliche Gerichts-Ordnung von 1726. M. Supplementen. Neue Aufl. Darmstadt, 1830. 3.50

136 **(Clairac, E.),** Us, et coustumes de la mer. De la navigation. Du commerce naval, contracts maritimes, et de la iurisdiction de la marine. Av. un traité des termes de marine. Revue et augm. etc. Bourdeaux, 1661, 60. 2 vols. in 1. 4to. limp vellum. 50.—

137 **Clarus Alexandrinus, J.,** Opera omnia, sive practica civilis atque criminalis. Geneva, 1666. fol. vellum. 15.—

138 **Clausel de Coussergues,** Du sacre des rois de France, et des rapports de cette cérémonie avec la constitution de l'état aux différens ages de la monarchie. — Relations des cérémonies du sacre de Louis XIV. — Observations sur quelques points importans de l'histoire de France, relatifs au sacre de nos rois. Paris, 1825. 3 vols. in 1. Hfcalf. (back broken). 6.—

139 **Coccejus, S. de,** Jus civile controversum. Francof. 1740. 2 vols. 4to. vellum. 10.—

140 **Cochin, H.,** Oeuvres, contenant le recueil de ses mémoires et consultations. Paris, 1751–53. 4 vols. W. portrait. 4to. calf. 7.50

141 — — The same. Nouv. éd. Paris, 1747. 6 vols. 4to. calf. 10.—

142 **Code criminal** de l'empereur Charles V; vulgairement appellé la Caroline. Maestricht, 1779. 4to. calf. 4.—

143 **Códigos antiguos** de España. Coleccion completa....desde el fuero juzgo hasta la novísima recopilacion. Con glosario, notas, etc. publ. p. M. Martinez Alcubilla. Madrid, 1885. 1 vol. in 2. Spanish calf. 18.—

144 **Cohnfeldt, R.,** Die Lehre vom Interesse nach römischem Recht. Lpz. 1865. 1.25

145 **Coleccion** de todas las pragmaticas, cedulas, provisiones, circulares, etc. publ. en el reynado del Don Carlos IV. (1793–1800). Con notas instructiovas y curiosas. Por S. Sanchez. Madrid, 1794–1801. 3 vols. calf. 15.—

146 **Collecção chronologica da legislação Portugueza.** Compil. e annot. p. J. J. de Andrade e Silva, 1603–1700 e Suppl. 1641–83. Lisboa, 1855–59. 5 vols. fol. Hfcalf. 55.—

147 **Collecção da legislação Portugueza,** 1750–1820 e Suppl. 1750–1790. Red. p. A. Delgado da Silva. Lisboa, 1825–44. 8 vols. fol. 6 of which calf, and 2 hfcalf. (Bindings somewhat rubbed). 95.—

The Suppl. III (1791/1820) is missing.

148 **Collectanea** doctorum, Sacrae rotae decisionum, etc. ad concilium Tridentinum, authore H. Baldassinio. Aesii, 1761. fol. vellum. 3.50

149 **Collection** of about 900 theses (dissertationes) and about 400 tracts (disputationes), all in latin, on old german law, international law, „jus naturae'' and roman law, published between the years 1594 and 1780. Together upwards of 1300 pieces, bound in 50 stout vols. vellum 4to. and boards. 600.—

This very important collection, brought together at the end of the 18th century by Friedrich von Schorlemer (see: Allgem. Deutsche Biographie, vol. 54) contains principally works on german (and international) law published between 1700 and 1760.

150 **Conciolus, A.,** De haerede cui accesserunt consilia criminalia. No pl. (ab. 1757). fol. Hfvellum. (Titlepage missing.) 2.—

151 **Conciolus, A.,** Resolutiones criminales. — **Id.,** Allegationes forenses civiles et criminales. — etc. Ven. 1700. 3 vols. in 1. fol. vellum. 6.50

152 **Conrat (Cohn), M.,** Das Ashburnhamer Rechtsbuch. Quelle der Exceptiones Petri. Lpz. (1886). 1.—

153 — Geschichte der Quellen und Literatur des römischen Rechts im früheren Mittelalter. Lpz. 1889–91. Vol. I. Bound. 24.—

All published. Out of print.

154 — Breviarium Alaricianum. Römisches Recht im Fränkischen Reich in systemat. Darstellung. Lpz. 1903. 18.—

155 — Die Entstehung des Westgothischen Gaius. Amst. 1905. (Akad.) 5.—

156 — Der Westgothische Paulus. Rechtshistor. Untersuch. Amst. 1908. (Akad.) 7.50

157 **Consolato del mare. — Llibre de consolat** dels fets maritims. Barcelona, 1592. W. large woodcut on titlepage. fol.orig. limp vellum. 275.—

Edition in the original Catalan text of this famous book, the first edition of which appeared in 1484.

158 **Consolato, Il,** del mare; nel quale si comprendono tutti gli statuti et ordini: disposti da gli antichi, per ogni caso di mercantia e di navigare. Venetia, L. Spineda, 1599. — **(Gerardo, P.),** Il portolano del mare, nel qual si dichiara minutamente del sito di tutti i porti. Ibid, id. 1599. — In 1 vol. 4to. calf. 120.—

Several later editions in stock.

159 **Constitutiones** et decreta synodi dioecesanae Constantiensis. Edita ac promulgata.... 1609. Constantiae, 1609. 4to. vellum. (Uppermargin of titlepage repaired). 10.—

160 **Constitutions** y altres drets de Cathalunya compilats en virtut del cap.de Cort XXIIII de las Corts en la vila de Montso any 1585. Barcelona, H. Gotard, 1588–89. 3 vols. in one. fol. vellum. 95.—

Second edition of the collection of Constitutions of Catalonia; the first was published in 1495.

Very scarce. Two pp. of the index of the 1st part are missing.

161 — — The same. Barcelona, 1704. 3 vols. in 1. W. coats of arms on titlepage. fol. vellum. Stout vol. 90.—

This is the third edition. „Impresión correcta y en papel fuerte" (Palau). Tall copy. The last 3 leaves and the errata-leaf are missing, but replaced by manuscript (on old paper).

162 **Consuetudines** infra script. civitatum et provinc. Galliae: Bituricensis, N. Boerii; Aurelianensis, P. Englebermei; Turonensis, J. Sainsonii comment. ill. Rec. D. Gothofredus. Francof., N. Bassaeus, 1598. fol. vellum. 7.50

163 **Consuetudines Bruxellenses** (dutch text) lat. et gallice redditae, commentarius ac notes ill. K. B. Christijn. Brux. (ab. 1690). fol. calf. 12.—

163*a* **Coquille, G.,** Oeuvres, conten. plusieurs traitez touchant les libertez de l'église gallicane, l'histoire de France et le droit français. Bordeaux, 1703. 2 vols. fol. calf. 25.—

The best edition of this celebrated jurist of the 16th century.

Contains i.a.: Les coutumes du pays et comte de Nivernois.

164 **Coronis, F. de,** Recueil de consultations sur diverses matières. Paris, 1735. 2 vols. W. portrait. fol. calf. 24.—

165 **Coroleu, J., y J. Pella y Forgas,** Los fueros de Cataluña. Descripcion coment. de la constitucion histor. del principado; sus instituciones políticas y administrat. y sus libertades tradicionales, con la relacion de muchas revoluciones, etc. Barcelona, 1878. W. front. and 21 portraits and pl. fol. calf. 20.—

166 **Corpus** constitutionum Brandenburgensico-Culmbacensium, oder vollständige Sammlung der vornehmsten in dem Marggrafthume Brandenburg-Culmbach.... Landes-Ordnungen und Gesetze. Bayreuth, 1746–48. 2 vols. in 3. W. portrait and front. 4to. boards. 20.—

167 **Corpus** constitutionum Magdeburgicarum novissimorum, oder Königl. Preusz. und Churfl. Brandenb. Landes-Ordnungen, edicta und mandata, im Hertzoghtum Magdeburg, 1680–1714. Mit „Continuatio" von C. O. Mylius, 1714–1717. Magdeburg, (1714, 18). 7 vols. in 1. W. portrait. 4to. calf. 40.—

168 **Corpus juris canonici.** C. notis ill. indicibus et appendice P. Lancellotti. Colon. Munat. 1682. 4to. vellum. (back slightly damaged). 5.—

169 **Corpus** juris confoederationis Germanicae oder vollständige Sammlung der Quellen der deutschen Bundesrechts vom Lüneviller Frieden bis zu den neuesten Bundesgesetzen. Hrsg. von G. v. Meyer. Frankfurt, 1822. 2 vols. in 1. boards. 5.—

170 **Corpus juris Sueo-Gotorum antiqui.** Samling af Sveriges gamla lagar. M. Ordbok. Utg. af H. S. Collin och C. J. Schlyter. Stockholm, 1827–77. 12 vols. 4to. boards and sewn. 125.—

171 **Corvinus, A.,** Iurisprudentiae Romanae summarium. Amst., L. et D. Elsevir, 1655, 60. 2 vols. in 1. 4to. calf. 5.—
Willems, no. 1183.
172 **Coscus, C.,** De sponsalibus filiorumfamilias .s vota decisiva. Romae, 1763. fol. vellum. 3.—
173 — — The same. Romae, 1766. fol. boards. 3.—
174 **Costa, J. B.,** De portione rata. Renov. ed. Ven. 1610. fol.vellum. 6.—
175 **Costumen** der stede van Audenaerde. Ghendt, I. van der Steene, 1615. 4to. vellum. 12.50
176 **Costumen** d. stede, casselrye enz. v. Berghen St. Winnocx. Ghendt, 1643. 4to. calf. 8.50
Interleaved, with numerous annotations.
177 **Costumen** ende wetten van Ghendt. M. de notulen van L. v. d. Hane. Gendt, 1765. calf. 2.50
178 — — The same. Gendt, 1779. calf. 3.50

COUTUMIERS

179 **Berroyer, C.,** et **E. de Lauriere,** Bibliothèque des coutumes, cont.: préface d'un nouveau coutumier général; liste hist. des coutumiers généraux; liste alphab. des textes et commentaires des coutumes; textes des anciennes et des nouvelles coutumes de Bourbonnois. Paris, 1699. 4to. calf. (back slightly damaged). 20.—
180 **Bourjon, F.,** Le droit commun de la France, et la coutume de Paris. Paris, 1747. 2 vols. fol. calf. (Binding damaged). 20.—
181 **Ferriere, C. J. de,** Dictionnaire de droit et de pratique, conten. l'explication des termes de droit, d'ordonnances, de coutumes etc. Avec les jurisdictions de France. Nouv. éd. augm. Toulouse, 1779. 2 vols. 4to. calf. 12.—
182 **Lorgnier, L.,** Les cateux dans les coutumes du Nord de la France. Paris, 1906. 2.50
183 **Milles de Souvigny, J.,** Style et pratique fondez et adaptez aux ordonnances royaux et coutumes de France. Lyon, 1556. W. portrait. fol. limp vellum. 40.—
184 **Coustumes, Les,** et statuz particuliers de la pluspart des bailliages, seneschaucees, etc. de France, arrestees.... par le roy, et de nouveau deuement collationnées aux registres de la cour du Parlement. Av.plusieurs autres coustumes non accordees.... Et de nouvel le coustumier de la marche etc. Paris, J. Petit, 1527. W. title in red and black, woodcut on v°, repeated on the last leaf and printer's mark at the end. sm. fol. full green mor., back and sides richly ornamented, gilt edges. 150.—
Very early edition of the Coutumes de France. Excessively rare.
The lower margin of the titlepage and a few leaves carefully repaired. Otherwise a very fine copy in excellent condition.
185 **Coustumes générales et particuliéres** de France et des Gaules. Corr. et annot. p. Ch. du Moulin e.a. Augm. et-rev. p. G. Michel. Paris, 1635. 2 vols. fol. calf. 35.—
186 **Coutumier général, Nouveau,** ou corps des costumes générales et particul. de France. Publ. p. Bourdout de Richebourg. Paris, 1724. 4 vols. fol. calf. (Binding slightly damaged). 45.—

187 **Amiens. — Coustumes generale** du bailliage d'Amiens. Comment. p. A. de Heu. Paris, 1653. W. portrait. folio. calf. 25.—
188 **Angoulème. — Coutumes, Les,** du pais et duché d'Angoumois. Aumis et gouvernement de La Rochelle. Av. comment. de J. Vigier. 2e éd. corr. et augm. des additions de J. Vigier. Angoulême, 1720. fol. calf. (Titlepage mended.). 25.—
189 — **Coutume** d'Angoumois, commentée et conférée avec le droit commun du royaume de France; par E. Souchet. Paris, 1780, 83. 2 vols. 4to. calf. 18.—
190 **Anjou. — Coustume d'Anjou. — Delomeau, P.,** Deux livres de la jurisprudence françoise, avec remarques et decisions notables, etc..... Le tout rapporté sur chacun article de la coustume d'Anjou. Saumur, 1605. 2 vols. in 1. sm. folio. Hfcalf. (Mod. binding). 35.—
Scarce. A third book was published in 1607.
One margin of the titlepage repaired. A few leaves slightly waterstained.
191 — **Coustumes** du pays et duché d'Anjou. Avec le comment. de G. Dupineau. Nouv. éd. par C. Pocquet de Livonniere. Paris, 1725. 2 vols. Without the portrait. fol. calf. 35.—

192 **Arras. — Coutumes locales,** tant anciennes que nouvelles de la loy, banlieue et échevinage d'Arras, de Bapaume, de Lens et du pays de l'Alloeu. Paris, 1746. 4to. 7.50
193 **Artois. — Coutumes** générales d'Artois avec des notes p. A. Maillart. Paris, 1704. 4to. calf. (A few wormholes). 15.—
194 **Auvergne. — Coustumes** du Haut et Bas pays d'Auvergne. Avec paraphrase de J. de Basmaison Pougnet et notes de Ch. du Moulin. 4e éd. augm. Clermont, 1667. 2 vols. in 1. 4to. calf. (Binding damaged). 15.—
Some pages with marginal annotations.
195 — **Coutumes** du haut et bas pais d'Auvergne, conférées avec le droit civil et avec les coutumes de Paris, de Bourbonnois, de la Marche, de Berri, et de Nivernois. Avec les notes de Ch. du Moulin. Paris, 1695. 4to. calf. (Name on titlepage). 15.—
196 — — The same. Nouv. éd. augm. des notes de Toussaint Chauvelin, e.a. Clermont-Ferrand, 1770. 4to. calf. 20.—
197 **Bar-le-Duc. — Le Paige, J.,** Nouveau commentaire sur la coutume de Bar-le-Duc conferée avec celle de St. Michiel, dont le texte est joint. 2e éd. rev. corr. et augm. de notes. Bar-le-Duc, 1711. calf. (A small hole in titlepage). 7.50
198 **Beauvoisis. — Beaumanoir, Ph. de,** Coustumes de Beauvoisis. Assises et bons usages du royaume de Jérusalem par J. d'Ibelin et autres anc. coutumes. Av. notes et observ. p. G. Th. de Thaumassière. Bourges, 1690. 2 vols. in 1. fol. calf. 15.—
199 — — — The same. Nouv. éd. p. Beugnot. Paris, 1842. 2 vols. Hfcalf. 15.—
200 **Berry. — Consuetudines** generales Bituricenses, Turonenses ac Aurelianenses. Cum glossemate ab N. Boerii, J. Sainson ac P. Englebermaeo. Parisiis, F. Regnault, 1529. 4to. calf. (Binding damaged). 60.—
The first edition containing the customs of Berry, Tours and Orleans together. Text in french with latin comments.
201 — **Consuetudines** Bituricenses praesidatuum, seu si mavis balliviatuum, cum fertilissimo utilium.... materiarum glossemate, consuetudines ipsas non parum exornante, à Nic. Boerio decisae. Aurelianenses praesid. à Pyrrho Englebermeo enucleatae. Turonenses praesid. à J. Sainson. Paris, G. Pratensis, 1543. 3 parts in 1 vol. 4to. full red mor., dentelles borders, gilt edges. (*Capé*). *Fine, tall copy.* 100.—
Text in french, the notes in latin.
202 — **Coustumes, Les,** générales des pays et duché de Berry. Avec le commentaire, et conférence des autres coustumes et statuts de France, par F. Ragneau. Paris, 1615. fol. calf. (Binding repaired). 24.—
203 — **Thaumas de la Thaumassière, G.,** Nouveaux commentaires sur les coutumes generales des pays et duché de Berri. Nouv. éd. Av. le traité du Franc-aleu de Berri. Bourges, 1701. fol. calf. (Binding damaged). 15.—
204 **Bordeaux. — Ferron, A.,** Appendix ad comment. in consuetudines Burdigalensium, Lemovicis, G. Nobalius, 1546. Hfvellum. (Mod. binding). 30.—
Very scarce impression of Limoges.
205 — **Automne, B.,** Commentaire sur les coutumes générales de la ville de Bordeaux et pays Bourdelois. Bordeaux, 1728. fol. calf. (Binding damaged). 24.—
206 **Bourbonnais. — Coutumes** generales et locales de Bourbonnais, avec le commentaire, p. M. Auroux des Pommiers. Paris, 1732. — **Additions** au nouveau commentaire etc. Paris, 1741. — Tog. 4 vols. in 1. fol. calf. 40.—
Scarce with the Additions.
207 **Bourgogne. — Chasseneus, Barth. a,** Tertia recognitio commentariorum in Consuetudines ducatus Burgundie precipue, ac totius Gallie secundario. (*At the end:*) Lugduni, Ant. du Ry, 1528. W. woodcut op the titlegpage (1× repeated) and some pedigrees. — **Repertorium** seu mavis index in commentaria Bart. de Chasseneus super consuetudinibus Burgundie. Ibid., id., 1528. W. title surrounded by a woodcut border. — 4to. calf. (modern binding). 60.—
Second edition of the much reprinted commentary of Bartholomaeus a Chasseneo. The last leaf of the commentary and one corner of the titlepage of the Repertorium carefully repaired.
208 — — Commentarii in consuetudines ducatus Burgundiae, feréque totius Galliae, multo emendat. Lugduni, B. Vincentius, 1574. folio. calf. 40.—
209 — **Coutumes** générales et locales du pays et duché de Bourgonnois. Av. comment. et notes de Ch. Dumoulin e.a. Par M. A. de Pommiers. Ajouté les anciennes coutumes. Riom, 1780. 2 vols. in 1. fol. calf. (Binding damaged). 25.—
210 — **Coutume** générale des pays et duché de Bourgogne. Av. comment. de Taisand. Dijon, 1698. fol. calf. 18.—

211 **Bourgogne. — Coutume, La,** du duché de Bourgogne, enrichie des remarques de Ph. de Villers, J. de Pringles, et J. Guillaume. Ensemble l'Histoire de tous les commentatuers. Dijon, 1717. 4to. calf. 15.—

212 — **Coutumes, Les,** de Bourgogne avec les anciennes coutumes et les observat. de Bouhier. Dijon, 1742. 46. 2 vols. fol. calf. (Bindings slightly damaged). 45.—

213 — **Champeaux, E.,** La compilation de Bouhier et les coutumiers bourguignons du XIVe siècle. Le coutumier bourguignon de Montpellier (Ms. H. 386). Paris, 1907. 1.50

Collection de textes rel. au droit et aux institutions de la Bourgogne.

214 — **Robin, H.,** Le droit des gens mariés dans la coutume du duché de Bourgogne. Paris, 1900. 4.50

215 **Braband. — Coutumes** du pays et duché de Brabant, publ. p. A. de Cuyper et C. Casier. (Texte néerl. et française traduct. moderne). Brux. 1869, 73. 2 vols. 4to. Hfcalf. 25.—

I. Coutumes de la ville de Bruxelles. — II. Coutumes diverses.
Forms a part of the Recueil des anciens coutumes de la Belgique.

216 **Bretagne. — Coustumes generales** du pais et duche de Bretagne. Revues et corrigées sur l'original de 1539. Adjectae sunt Cl. et Pr. V. ex jure civili efforo notae. Rennes, J. du Clos, 1568. 4to. limp vellum. 30.—

217 — **Bigotière, R. de la,** Commentaire sur la coutume de Bretagne. 2e éd. rev. et augm. Rennes, 1702. 4to. calf. 7.50

218 — **Coutumes** générales du païs et duché de Bretagne. Rennes, 1745–48. 3 vols. 4to. calf. (Librarystamp on titlepage). 32.—

219 — **Coutume de Bretagne, La très ancienne,** avec les assises, constitutions de parlement et ordonnances duciles, suivies d'un recueil de textes divers antérieurs à 1491. Ed. acc. de notices par M. Planiol. Rennes, 1896. 6.—

Bibliothèque bretonne armoricaine, II.

220 **Cambrai. — Coutumes** generales de la ville et duché de Cambray, pays et conté du Cambresis. Av. explication etc. par Pinault des Jaunaux. Douay, 1691. 4to. calf. 12.—

221 **Chartres. — Coustumes, Les,** du duché et baillage de Chartres, pays chartrain, Perche-Gouet. Avec les commentaires de Ch. du Moulin, G. Tulove et N. Frerot. Paris, 1604. 4to.limp vellum. 25.—

222 — **Coutumes** de Chartres, pays Chartrain, etc. Comm. p. J. Couart. 2e éd. Augm. des notes de C. du Molin. Chartres, 1687. calf. 12.—

223 **Chateau-Neuf. — Coustumes voisines, Les trois,** de Chasteau-Neuf, Chartres, et Dreux. Avec les notes de Ch. Du Moulin et Du Laurens. Chartres, 1645. 4to. vellum. 15.—

224 **Chaumont. — Coutume** de Chaumont en Bassigny. Nouv. commentée, etc. par J. Delaistre. Paris, 1733. 4to. calf. 15.—

225 **Evreux. — Coutumier, Ancien,** de l'église cathédrale d'Evreux, vulgairement appelé Hunaud, publ. p. F. Blanquart. 1906. *Reprint.* 3.50

226 **Franche Comté. — Ordonnances** de prince Charles V, publ. à Dole. Reveuës et augm. Dole, J. Droz, 1570. — **Recueil** d'aucuns edicts, statuts, etc. publiez et observez au conté de Bourgoigne. Ausquels sont adioustez deux mandements du roy, contre les recelateurs des biens rebelles, etc. Ibid., id., 1570. — **Ordonnances** de prince Philippe. Roy des Espaignes publ. à Dole, 1586. Lyon, J. d'Ogerolles, 1586. — Tog. 3 vols. in 1. folio. Hfcalf. (back damaged). 35.—

Scarce collections of ordonnances of the Franche-Comté and Bourgogne.
The titlepage of the last work is lacking. Some pages a little waterstained.

227 — **Recueil** des ordonnances et édits de la Franche-Comté de Bourgongne(*sic*). Par J. Petremand. Dole, 1619. — **Les coustumes générales** de la Franche-Comté de Bourgongne(*sic*). Id. 1619. — **Suite** du Recueil des édits. Lyon, 1664. — **Abrégé** des édits, ordonnances et coutumes de la Franche-Comté. Lyon, 1664. — In 1 vol. fol. calf. 25.—

228 **La Marche. — Coutumes** de la province et comté pairie de La Marche, ressort du parlement de Paris. On a joint toutes les ordonnances, édits, etc. de Louis XV par Couturier de Fournone. Clermont-Ferrand, 1744. calf. 8.—

229 **La Rochelle. — Commentaire, Nouveau,** sur la coutume de La Rochelle et du pays d'Aunis. Publ. par R. J. Valin. La Rochelle, 1756. 3 vols. 4to. calf. 28.—

230 **Lille. — Coustumes et usages** generaulx et particuliers de la salle, bailliage et chastellenie de Lille, confirmez par sa Maiesté. Douay, L. de Winde, on les vend a Lille par D. Boulet, 1569. W. coats of arms on v° of the titlepage and woodcut portrait of Philips II. 4to. full polished mor., inside border, gilt edges. *Fine copy.* 75.—

Early edition of the „Coutumes de Lille", being one of the first products of the Douay presses. Extremely scarce.

231 **Lille.** — **Patou, F.,** Commentaire sur les coutumes de Lille et de sa châtellenie et conférences av. celles voisines et le droit commun. Lille, 1788–90. 3 vols. fol. Hfcalf. 20.—

232 **Lorraine.** — **Coustumes** generales de Lorraine, es baillages, de Nancy, Vosges et Allemagne. Nancy, 1614. — **Recueil** du stile à observer es instructions des procedures d'assizes, es baillages de Nancy, etc. Ibid. 1614. — 2 vols. in 1. 4to. limp vellum. (Somewhat waterstained). 18.—

233 **Loudunois.** — **Le Proust, P.,** Commentaires sur les coustumes du pays de Loudunois. Saumur, Th. Portau, 1612. limp vellum. 20.—

234 — **Coustumes** du pays et seigneurii de Lodunoys. Poictiers, Bouchetz, no d. (ab. 1650?) sm. 8vo. vellum. 20.—

Interleaved, with numerous annotations in old ms. The titlepage a little soiled bearing the names of several previous owners.

Scarce.

235 **Maine.** — **Coustumes, Ce sont les,** du pays et conte du Mayne, publiées pat Thibault Baillet et Jehan le Lieure, etc. (*At the end:*) Imprimees a Paris lan 1519. sm. 4to. calf. (binding a little damaged). 35.—

Probably the third edition of the customs of Maine, not mentioned by the bibliographers. Extremely rare.

Our copy lacks the titlepage (which is replaced by that of the edition of 1554 in facs.) and perhaps 2 blank leaves at the end. The margin of the first leave repaired, otherwise a very well preserved copy.

236 — **Coustumier, Le grant,** du pays et comté du Maine. Auquel est le texte dicelluy en francoys. Avec la glose, additions, etc. par G. le Rouille Dalençon. Paris, F. Regnault, 1535. W. title surrounded by a woodcut border. fol. old calf. (Back broken). 75.—

237 — **Coustumes, Les,** du pays et conté du Maine. Nouv. reveneuës. Le Mans, H. Olivier, 1607. sm. 8vo. calf. 15.—

238 **Metz.** — **Coûtumes generales** de la ville de Metz et pays Messin. 2e éd. Metz, 1688. 12mo. calf. 6.—

239 — **Coutumes** generales de la ville de Metz et pays Messin. Enrichies d'un commentaire. 2e éd. Metz, 1732. calf. (Corners repaired). 10.—

240 — **Coutumes** generales de la ville de Metz et pays Messin. Enrichies d'un commentaire. Metz, 1730. 4to. calf. 15.—

241 — **Jager, F.,** De la transmission héréditaire des biens d'après la coutume de Metz et pays messin. Paris, 1911. 3.—

242 **Namur.** — **Coutumes** de Namur et coutume de Philippeville, p. J. Grandgagnage. Brux. 1869, 74. 2 vol. 4to. Hfcalf. 25.—

Forms a part of: Recueil des anciennes coutumes de la Belgique.

243 **Nivernois.** — **Coustumes** du pays et duché de Nivernois. Avec annot. et commentaires de G. Coquille. Paris, 1705. 4to. limp vellum. 24.—

244 **Normandy.** — **Coustumier, Le grant,** du pays et duche de Normendie.... enquel est le texte diceluy en francois avec la glose ordinaire et familiere. Et mesmes y est le texte en latin.... Et le repertoire, ... la charte aux normans, ... les traictez de sanguinite. Item .... les ordonnances royaulx .... Item le stille de proceder fait a Rouen le 21 janvier, 1515. Nouv. imprimé à Rouen pour J. Richard, (1515). W. title in red and black. fol. blind stamped leather. (Mod. binding). 150.—

Extremely scarce edition of the customs of Normandy. „Edition fort rare". (Brunet).

Very well preserved copy in a modern binding.

„Le stille de proceder" and the „Tractatus arboris consanguineitatis" are bound between ll. 124 and 125.

245 — **Coustumier, Le grand,** du pays et duché de Normendie. Avec plusieurs additions par G. le Rouille. Aussi y est le texte en latin.... la chartre aux normands, ... toutes les ordonnances royaulx...., le stille de proceder. Rouen, N. le Roux, 1539. W. title surrounded by a woodcut border. folio. vellum. (Modern binding). 75.—

Very scarce.

246 — **Terrien, G.,** Commentaires du droict civil tant public que privé, observé au pays et duché de Normandie, ... coustume dudict duché, etc. Le tout en texte et engloses. Paris, 1574. folio. calf. (728 pp.). 40.—

First edition.

247 — **Coustumes** du pays de Normandie, anciens ressors, et enclaves d'iceluy. Paris, J. du Pays, 1587. 4to. limp vellum. 35.—

Early edition. Scarce.

248 — — The same. L'Isle, G. des Marescs, 1589. sm. 8vo. Hfvellum. (Mod. binding). 20.—

249 **Normandy.** — **Coutume** reformée du païs et duché de Normandie. Commentée par H. Basnage .2e éd. Rouen, 1697. 2 vols. fol. calf. 24.—

250 — **Coutume** de Normandie. Expl. p. Pesnelle. 2e éd. Rouen, 1727. 4to. calf. (Binding damaged). 12.—

251 — — The same. 4e éd. avec observations de Roupnel de Chenilly. Rouen, 1771. 2 vols. 4to. calf. (Binding slightly damaged). 18.—

252 — **Commentaires** sur la coutume de Normandie, par Bérault, Godefroy et d'Aviron. Nouv. éd. Rouen, Paris, 1776. 2 vols. fol. calf. 30.—

253 — **Fessard, M.,** La capacité civile de la femme mariée en droit normand et en droit anglais. Paris, 1914. (Several words underlined). 4.50

254 — **Flaust, J. B.,** Explication de la coutume et de la jurisprudence de Normandie. Rouen, 1781. 2 vols. fol. Hfcalf. 40.—

255 — **Houard, D.,** Traités sur les coutumes anglo-normandes, publ. en Angleterre, depuis le 11e jusqu'au 14e siècle. Rouen, 1776. 4 vols. With fine portrait of Louis XVI. 4to. Hfcalf. 50.—

„Ouvrage bien fait et fort curieux." (*Brunet*).
The vols. I–III are in latin, vol. IV in old french.

256 — — Dictionnaire analyt., histor., (et) étymolog. de la coutume de Normandie. Rouen, 1780–82. 4 vols. 4to. Hfcalf. 24.—

257 — **Marnier, M. A. J.,** Etablissements et coutumes, assises et arrêts de l'échiquier de Normandie au 13e siècle. (1207–1245). Paris, 1839. Hfcalf. 4.50

258 **Orleans.** — **Coustumes** des duché, bailliage, etc. d'Orléans. Mises et redigées p. A. de Harlay, J. Viole, et N. Perrot. Orleans, S. Hottot, 1583. 4to. calf. 20.—

259 — **Coutume** d'Orléans. Comment. par Delalande. 2e éd. Orléans, 1704, 05. 2 vols. fol. calf, gilt back. 28.—

260 — **Coutumes....** d'Orléans. Av. introd. et notes. Orleans, 1760. 3 vols. in 2 sm. 8vo. calf. 10.—

261 — — The same. Accomp. de notes p. Pothier. Paris, 1772. 4to. calf. 20.—

262 — — The same. Nouv. éd. Paris, 1776. 2 vols. sm. 8vo. calf. 12.—

263 **Paris.** — **Coustumes** de la prevosté et vicomté de Paris, mises et redigées par Chr. de Thou, C. Anjorrant, e.a. Paris, J. du Prins, 1581. 4to. pigskin. (Mod. binding). 40.—

Interleaved, with several annotat. in old ms.

264 — **Coustumes** de la prevosté et vicomté de Paris. Avec les notes de C. du Moulin. Paris, 1665. sm. 8vo. calf. 6.50

265 — **Coustume** de la prevosté et vicomté de Paris, commentée par J. Brodeau. 2e éd. augm. Paris, 1669. 2 vols.fol. calf. 25.—

266 — **Duplessis,** Traités sur la coutume de Paris. 2e éd. Avec de notes de Berroyer et de Laurière. Paris, 1702. 2 vols. in 1. fol. calf. 15.—

267 — **Le Maistre, P.,** Coûtume de la prevosté et vicomté de Paris. Avec la resolution des questions que l'ambiguité du texte ont fait naistre. Paris, 1700. fol. calf. (Binding damaged). 18.—

268 — **Martin, O.,** La coutume de Paris. Trait d'union entre le droit roman et les législations modernes. Paris, 1925. 1.—

269 **Poitou.** — **Rat, P.,** In patrias Pictonum leges, quas vulgas consuetudines dicit, glossemata. Pictavii, Marnef, 1548. 4to. calf. 40.—

The titlepage and the margins of some 20 leaves repaired.

270 — — In Pictonum leges, quas vulgus consuetudines dicit, glossemata. Augustoriti Pictonum. (Poitiers), 1609. W. engraved titlepage. 4to. limp vellum. 30.—

„Coutumes de Poitou" with latin comments.

271 — **Coustumes** du comté et pays de Poictou, anciens ressorts et enclaves diceluy. Av. annot., p. J. Barraud. Poictiers, 1625. 4to. vellum. 18.—

272 — **Coutumier** général, ou compilation de tous les commentateurs sur la coutume de Poitou. Av. conférences, observat. et les notes de Ch. du Moulin. Par J. Boucheul. Poitiers, 1727. 2 vols. W. portrait. fol. calf. (1 binding damaged). 30.—

273 **Provence.** — **Statuts et coustumes** du pays de Provence. Comment. p. J. Morgues. Aix, 1642. 4to. limp vellum. 15.—

274 **Rheims.** — **Coustumes** de la cité et ville de Rheims, villes et villages regis selon icelles. Avec les comment. par J. B. de Buridan. Paris, 1665. W. portrait. fol. calf. 24.—

275 **Saint-Amand.** — **Coutume, La,** de Saint-Amand-en-Pévèle. Edition critique et commentaire par H. Raviart. Lille, 1907. 3.50

276 **St. Jean-d'Angely.** — **Coutume** du siege royal de St. Jean d'Angely en Saintonge. Comm. p. C. Bechet. Ens. la conference de l'usance de Saintes, etc. Saintes, 1689. 4to. limp vellum. 12.—

277 **Saint-Martin. — Recueil** de chartes et documents. de Saint-Martin-des-Champs, monastère parisien. (Publ.) par J. Depoin. Paris, 1912–21. 5 vols. (Archives de la France monastique t. 13, 16, 18, 20, 21). 20.—

278 **Saint-Mihiel. — Coutumes** du bailliage de Saint-Mihiel. Avec les ordonnances faites sur le stile et règlement de la justice au siège dudit bailliage. Metz, B. Antoine, 1698. 12mo. calf. 7.50

A few leaves of the „Epistre" are missing.

279 **Senlis. — Coûtumes** du bailliage de Senlis, et son ancien ressort. Avec des commentaires de J. M. Ricard et L. Bouchel. Paris, 1703. 4to. calf. 15.—

280 **Sens. — Coutume** des baillages de Sens et de Langres. Commentée p. J. de Laistre. Paris, 1731. 4to. calf. 20.—

281 **Toulouse. — Consuetudines Tolosae,** c. declarationibus in quibus consuetudines. Ipsae a iuris communis dispositione discrepare seu differre videantur.... C. interpr. et quaestion. J. de Casaveteri. Tolosae, Lud. Yuernaige, 1544. 4to. calf. *Scarce.* 50.—

282 **Touraine. — Consuetudines** totius presidatus seu Turonensis bailliuie. Cum glossemate s. commento Joh. Sainxon.... (*At the end:*) Imprimé a Paris par Jacques Poussin pour Hylaire malicam.... et pour Jehan margerie.... libraire a tours, (1523). 4to. calf. (Back somewhat broken). 80.—

Early edition of the Coustumes de Touraine, of great rarity, containing the french text with latin comments.

Ms. exlibris on the titlepage and an insignificant wormhole in the text. Otherwise in excellent condition.

283 — **Coustumes** du duché et bailliage de Touraine. Av. annot. d'E. Pallu. Tours, 1661. 4to. calf. 20.—

284 **Troyes. — Coutume** du bailliage de Troyes. Av. comment. de L. Le Grand. Paris, 1714. fol. calf. (Titlepage missing). 2.50

285 — **Coutume** du bailliage de Troyes. Av. comment. de L. Le Grand. 2e éd. Paris, 1715. fol. calf. 15.—

286 — — The same. 4e éd. Paris, 1737. fol. calf. 25.—

287 **Vermandois. — Coustumes generales** du baillage de Vermandois, en la cité et prevosté Foraine de Laon, et les particuliers de Ribemont, Sainct Chuentin, Noyon, et Coucy. Avec comment. p. J. B. Buridan. Reims, N. Hicart, 1630. sm. 4to. calf. 24.—

288— **Coûtumes** du baillage de Vermandois. Av. notes p. C. de la Fons. Nouv. éd. Metz, 1688. 12mo. calf. (back damaged). 8.—

289 — **Coutumier, Le,** de Vermandois, conten. les comment. de Buridan, La Fons et D'Hericourt, de Godet et Billecart sur Chalons, de Buridan sur Rheims, de Vrevin sur Chaulny. Paris, 1728. 2 vols. calf. fol. 30.—

290 — **Coustumes** des pays de Vermendois et ceulx de envyron. Publ. par C. J. Beautemps-Beaupré. Paris, 1858. 5.—

291 **Vitry. — Coutumes** du bailliage de Vitry en Perthois. Av. commentaire p. E. Durand. Chaalons, 1722. fol. calf. 25.—

292 **Covarruvias, D.,** In quartum decretalium librum epitome. Item de testamentis et constit. Bonifacii VIII, ultima, quae incipit, Alma mater, interpretatio. Lugdini, J. Junta, 1558. boards. (550 pp.) 10.—

293 **Cramer, J. U. von,** Wetzlarische Beiträge aus der Reichs-Praxi dasigen höchsten Reichs-Gerichts. Wetzlar, 1763. Vol. I (all published). sm. 8vo. calf. 4.—

294 **Cucchus, M. A., A. Rubeus, C. de Battandier, e.a.** De legitima et quae ad eandem materiam pertinent. Neostad, M. Harnisius, 1594. vellum. (Librarystamp on titlepage). 5.—

295 **Cujacius, J.,** Opera ab ipso auct. rec. Ed. 3a. Francof. 1623. 4 vols. in 1. fol. vellum. 3.50

296 — Opera omnia, cur. C. A. Fabroti. Acc. Graeca versio locorum, index locupl. etc. Neapoli, 1722–27. 11 vols. W. portrait. fol. calf. 90.—

Very valuable edition.

297 — Ad Africanum reliqui tractatus VI–IX. Eiusd. Observat. 11. XII, XIII, XIV. Lugd., C. Senneton, 1573. fol. 6.—

298 **Cutellus, M.,** De donationibus contemplatione matrimonii, aliisque de causis inter parentes et filios factis. Ven. 1661. 2 vols. in 1. fol. vellum. 3.50

299 — — The same. Ed. 2a. Ven. 1668. 2 vols. in 1. fol. vellum. 5.—

300 **Cuypers, P. en G.,** Tractaet van grondt-proceduren ofte vande uyt-werckinghe vande actie hypothecaire.... volgens den styl ende costuyme van Mechelen. Mechelen, 1679. 4to. calf. 7.50

301 **Cyriacus, T. N.,** Controversiae forenses. Ven. 1664. 4 vols. fol. Hfvellum. 12.
302 **Damhouder, J.,** Opera omnia, c. notis N. Thuldeni. Antw. 1646. fol. vellum. 40.—
303 **Daniel de Nobilibus,** Disputationes. Senis, 1645. 4to. vellum. 6.—
304 **Dareau, F.,** Traité des injures dans l'ordre judiciaire. Paris, 1776. sm. 8vo. Hfcalf. 4.—

Pp. 185–212: Des injures concernant les gens de lettres (Voltaire e.a.).

305 — — The same. Paris, 1777. sm. 8vo. calf. 3.50
306 **David, H. v.,** Zur Lehre der sogen. Ersitzungstitel nach Röm. Rechte. Wien, 1869. Bound. 1.—
307 **Davot, G.,** Traités sur diverses matières de droit françois, à l'usage du duché de Bourgogne, et des autres pays qui ressortissent au Parlement de Dyon. Av. notes de J. Bannelier. 2e éd. Av. add. de F. Petitot. Dyon, 1688–89. 4 vols. 4to. Hfcalf. 24.—
308 **Decisiones rote** nove ac antique cum margin. addition. Lugd., J. Bragneyrac, 1531. Title in woodcutborder. 4to. calf. 28.—
309 **Deckher, J.,** Dissertationes juris et decisiones posthumae in magnis supremisque consiliis.... in Belgio. Brux. 1673. fol. calf. 5.—
310 **Defacqz, E.,** De la paix du sang ou paix à partie dans les anciennes coutumes Belgiques. Brux. 1866. *Reprint.* 1.—
311 **Deleuze-Lancizolle, E.,** Droit romain. Des réformes apportées dans le régime successoral romain pour augmenter les droits de la famille. Droit français. Effets des actes du capitaine à l'égard du capitaine lui-même, de l'armateur et des propriétaires de marchandises. Paris, 1894. 5.—
312 **Delpit, J.,** Réponse d'un campagnard à un Parisien, ou réfutation du livre de Veuillot sur le droit du seigneur. Paris, 1857. 4.—
313 **Dernusson,** Traité des propres réels, reputez réels et conventionnels, oû sont traitées les notables questions du droit français. 3e éd. Paris, 1714. 4to. calf. 4.50
314 **Des Marez, G.,** Etude sur la propriété foncière dans les villes du moyen-age et spécialement en Flandre. Gand, 1898. W. 2 maps. Hfmor. (Recueil des travaux publ. p. la faculté de phil. et lettres, no. 20). 10.—
315 **(Desmarquets, Ch.),** Nouveau stile du châtelet de Paris, et de toutes les jurisdictions ordinaires du royaume, tant en matière civile, criminelle, que de police. Nouv. éd. Paris, 1762. 4to. calf. 6.—
316 **Didacus de Narbona,** Annales tractatus iuris de aetate ad omnes humanos actus requisita. Mantuae, 1642. fol. vellum. 6.50
317 **Dietzel, G.,** Das senatus consultum macedonianum. Lpz. 1856. boards. 1.25
318 **Diez Navarro, A.,** Alegacion fiscal, por el derecho, y regalias de la del real Aposento de Corte. No pl. (ab. 1740). fol. vellum. 9.50
319 **Differentiae** inter politicen genvinam ac diabolicam. Cum nonnullis actis publicis et articulis pacis inter ambas coronas initae. Ex Gallico transl. à J. Pastorio Juxta exemplar Amst. 1659. W. front. 12mo. vellum. 25.—
320 **Doneau. — Eyssel, A. P. Th.,** Doneau, sa vie et ses ouvrages. L'école de Bourges; synthèse du droit romain au XVIe siècle, etc. Trad. du lat. p. J. Simonnet. La Haye, 1860. 1.50
321 **Dukerus, C. A.,** Opuscula varia de latin. juris consult. veter. 2a ed. Ultr. 1761. sm. 8vo. vellum. 2.50
322 **Duncombe, G.,** Trials per pais; or, the law of England concern. juries by nisi prius, etc. W. treatise of the law of evidence.... forms of challenges, etc. 6th ed. (London), 1739. calf. (Binding damaged). 2.50
323 **Dunod de Charnage, F. I.,** Traités des prescriptions, de l'aliénation des biens d'église, et des dixmes, suivant les droits civil et canon. Paris, 1774. 4to. calf. 6.—
324 **Durand de Maillane,** Dictionnaire de droit canonique et de pratique bénéficiale. 2e éd. Lyon, 1770. 4 vols. 4to. calf. 15.—
325 — Institutes du droit canonique, traduites en français.... précédées de l'histoire du droit canon. Lyon, 1770. 10 vols. sm. 8vo. calf. 12.—

French-latin text.

326 **Duret, J.,** Alliance des loix romaines avec le droit françois contenu aux ordonnances des rois, arrests des cours souveraines et coustumes provincialles. Paris, 1600. 4to. Hfcalf. 10.—
327 **Dussert, A.,** Les états du Dauphiné aux 14e et 15e siècles. Grenoble, 1915. Bound. 6.—
328 **(Duval?),** Nouvelles institutions du droit françois. Par M***. Paris, 1733. sm. 8vo. calf. 3.50

329 **Eberstadt, R.,** Das französ. Gewerberecht und die Schaffung staatlicher Gesetzgebung und Verwaltung in Frankreich vom 13en Jahrh. bis 1581. Lpz. 1899. 4.50
Staats- und socialwissensch. Forsch. XVII, 2.

330 **Edits** de la république de Genève. Genève, 1707. 4to. calf. 10.—
Added: **(Ordonnance)** sur quelques nouveaux impots, 1718. — **Propositions** des citoyens (sur les élections).

331 **Eelking, J.,** De belgis sec. XII in Germaniam advenis variisq. institutis atq. jurib. ex eor. adventu ortis. Gött. 1770. 4to. boards. 2.50

332 **Eisenhart, J. F.,** De auctoritate et usu inscriptionum in jure. Helmst. 1750. 4to. 2.—

333 — Erzählungen von besonderen Rechtshändeln. Halle, 1768–83. 10 vols. boards. (Vol. I in 2d ed.) 24.—

334 **Eisen Ordnung.** — Röm. Khaiserl. [Maximilian II] .... newe Eisen-Ordnung unnd Satzung, auff Eisen und Stahl, so ausz dem Innerpergerischen rauchen Eisen geschmidt und Steyrisch Eisen genennt wirt. [Wien], C. Stainhofer, 1574. sm. fol boards. 45.—

335 **Ens, G.,** Nucleus-histor.-polit. Denuo recusus et 2 tract. auctus. I. Pharos-politicus principum. II. Pharos-politicus ministrorum. Col. 1625, 24. 2 vols. in 1. sm. 8vo. vellum 4.—

336 **Epistola gratulatoria** ad cardinales, inquisitorem gener. etc. de pontificia potest., inquisitionis jurisdict. et contradict. injustitia etc. Matrit. 1746. 4to. 2.—

337 **Ernst, V.,** Mittelfreie. Beitrag zur schwäbischen Standesgeschichte. Stuttg. 1920. 1.50

338 **Escobar, F. M. de,** De ratiociniis administratorum et computationibus variis aliis. Ursellae, 1620. fol. vellum. 5.—

339 **d'Espeisses, A.,** Oeuvres, où toutes les plus importantes matières du droit romain sont expliquées et acomodées au droit françois. 2e éd. Lyon, 1664. 3 vols. W. portr. fol. calf. (Bindings repaired). 15.—

340 — — The same. Nouv. éd. revue par G. du Rousseaud de la Combe. Lyon, 1750. 3 vols. fol. calf. 25.—

341 **Espen, Z. B. van,** Scripta omnia. Lovanii, 1753. 4 vols. fol. vellum. 40.—
I–II: Jus ecclesiasticum universum. — III. Comment. in canones juris veteris ac novi. — IV. Comment. in canones juris novi.
First collective and esteemed edition.

342 — Jus ecclesiast. univ. hodiernae disciplinae praes. Belgii, Galliae et vicinar. provinc. accomod. — **Id.,** Varia opuscula. — Lovan. 1700. 3 vols. fol. calf. 15.—

343 — Comment. in canones et decreta iuris veteris ac novi. Lovan. 1759. fol. vellum. 6.—

344 **Extraits analytiques** des anciens registres des consaux de Tournay, 1385–1430. Av. analyse des documents condern. le magistrat de 1211–1400. Publ. p. H. Vandenbroeck. Tournai, 1861, 63. 2 vols. 6.50

345 **Faber, A.,** Codex Fabrianus definitionum forensium, et rerum in Sacro Sabaudiae senatu tractatarum, ad ordinem Cod. Justin. Lugd. 1649. fol. calf. (Binding repaired, waterstained). 3.—

346 — — The same. Lugduni, 1681. fol. calf. 12.—

347 **Fachineus, A.,** Controversiarum juris ll. XIII. Col. Agr. 1649. 4to. vellum. 6.—

348 **Factum** pour les directeurs des villages du païs du Franc de de Bruges, au sujet des dixmes: contre les ecclésiastiques et autres, pretendans icelles dixmes. No pl. (1688). — **Réfutation** d'un imprimé intitulé i Factum etc. No pl. n. d. — Tog. 2 vols. fol. calf and hfcalf. 8.50

349 **(Faiguet de Villeneuve, J.),** Légitimité de l'usure légale, *ou* l'on prouve son utilité etc. Amst. 1770. sm. 8vo. (Waterstained). 2.—

350 **Farinacius, P.,** Consilia s. responsa atque decisiones causarum criminalium. Lugd. 1619. fol. vellum. 7.50

351 — De immunitate ecclesiarum et confugientibus ad eas. Appendix ad Quaest. XXVIII in Titulo de carceribus et carceratis. Romae, 1621. fol. vellum. 5.—

352 — — **Id.,** De furtis. — **Id.,** Fragment. crimin. Partes I, II. — etc. — Lugd. 1621, 29. Tog. 4 vols. in 1. fol. vellum (binding broken). 7.50

353 — Decisiones rotae Romanae, varias iuris, tum civilis, tum canonici decisiones continentes. Lugd. 1640. fol. vellum. 3.50

354 **Fauché-Prunelle, A.,** Essai sur les anciennes institutions, autonomes ou populaires des Alpes Cottiennes-Brionçonnaises. Grenoble, 1856. 2 vols. 3.50

355 **Fehr, H.,** Hammurapi und das Salische Recht. Bonn, 1910. 1.50

356 **Felicius, H.,** De societate. Ed. 2a. recogn. ab A. Felicio. Ven. 1610. fol. vellum. 3.—

357 **Feltman, G.,** De titulis honorum, ll. II. Bremae, 1672. 12mo. vellum. 2.50

358 **Feltman, G.** et **Th.,** Opera juridica. Ed. J. J. v. Hasselt. Arnhem, J. H. Moelemann, 1764–69. Vol. I–VII. 7 vols. fol. 12.—
359 **Ferraris, L.,** Prompta bibliotheca canonica, juridico-moralis theologica partim ascetica, polemica, etc. Bon. 1746. With index and suppl. 9 vols. 4to. vellum. (Inkspots on the titlepages). 15.—
360 — — (juris hispanici hodie etiam vocabitur). Opera Fr. M. Vallarna. Matr. 1786–88. 10 vols. in 5. fol. calf. 30.—
361 **Ferriere, C. de,** La jurisprudence du code de Justinian. conférée avec les ordonnances royaux, les coutumes de France, et les décisions des Cours souveraines. Paris, 1684. 2 vols. 4to. calf. 8.50
362 — Des droits de patronage, de présentation aux bénéfices de preseances des patrons, des seigneurs, et autres. Des droits honorifiques etc. Paris, 1686. 4to. calf. 6.—
363 **Ferrière, C. J. de,** Nouvelle introduction à la pratique, conten. l'explication des termes de pratique, de droit et de coutumes. Nouv. éd. Paris, 1758. 2 vols. sm. 8vo. calf. 7.50
364 **Ferron, J. P.,** Essai d'un système du droit coutumier luxembourgeois, précédé d'une introd. Luxemb. 1853. Hfmor. (Librarystamp on titlepage). 6.—
365 **Fevret, Ch.,** Traité de l'abus et du vrai sujet des appellations qualifiées du nom d'abus. Nouv. éd. augm. de notes. Lyon, 1736. 2 vols. W. portrait. fol. calf. 15.—
366 **Ficker, J.,** Ueber die Entstehungszeit des Sachsenspiegels und die Ableitung des Schwabenspiegels a. d. Deutschenspiegel. Innsbruck, 1859. Bound. 2.50
367 — Untersuchungen zur Erbenfolge der Ostgermanischen Rechte. Innsbruck, 1891–1904. Vol. I–IV, V, 1 and VI, 1. in 5 vols. Hfcloth. 45.—
All published. Out of print.
368 **Florens, Fr.,** Opera iuridica. Acc. tractatus duo: N. Januarius, De officio archi-diaconi et J. Fournet. De absolutione ad cautelam. Ven. 1763. fol. vellum. 4.50
369 **Fontanella, J. P.,** De pactis nuptialibus. Ven. 1645. 2 vols. fol. Hfvellum. 6.—
370 — — The same. Genevae, 1685. fol. calf. 6.—
371 **Forst-Ordnung, Erneuerte,** des Herzogthums Würtemberg, mit Constitutionibus und General-Rescripten. Stuttg. 1767. sm. 8vo. boards. 3.—
372 **Fragmentum** veteris jurisconsulti De juris speciebus et de manumissionibus. Gr.et Lat. Cur. M. Röver. Adj. observat. ad glossar. Lugd. Bat., C. Haak, 1739. boards. 2.50
373 **Franchis, J. F. de,** Vignolus restitutus s. praxis notariorum ad tract. contractuum et disposit. ultim. volunt. Lucae, 1721. fol. vellum. 4.—
374 **Freher,** De secretis judiciis olim in Westphalia aliisque Germaniae partibus usitatis. Cui acc. Joh. de Francfordia contra feymeros, tractatus. Heidelbergae, 1610. sm. 4to. old red morocco gilt. Fine copy. 24.—
375 **Freminville, E. de La Poix de,** Traité général du gouvernement des biens et affaires des communautés d'habitans des villes, bourgs, villages et paroisses du royaume. Paris, 1760. 4to. calf. 6.—
376 — La pratique universelle pour la rénovation des terriers et des droits seigneuriaux. Paris, 1762–77. 5 vols. 4to. calf. (Binding slightly damaged). 20.—
377 **Fritsch, A.,** Collection of 12 works. Jenae, etc. 1664–73. W. portrait. 4to. calf. 7.50
Contains: De jure at statu pagorum Germaniae. — Electa juris publici Romano-Germanici. — Tractatus de cambiis. — De dotatione filiae principis. — De jure archivi et cancellarae. — De conventibus provincialibus, von Landtägen. — De visitationibus provinc. Von Land-Visitationen. — De oblatione votorum. — De jure intradae, vulgo Einritt. — De jure praesidii vulgo Berathungs-Recht. — De jure optionis, etc.
378 — Corpus juris venatorio-forestalis. Jena, 1676. 3 parts in 1 vol. W. front. fol. vellum. 24.—
379 **Fulgineus, F.,** De iure emphyteutico. Ven. 1663. fol. vellum. 5.—
380 **Furgole, J. B.,** Oeuvres complètes. Paris, 1775–76. 8 vols. Bound. 15.—
I–IV. Traité des testamens, etc. — V. Traité de la Seigneurie féodale universelle et du franc-allen naturel. — VI. Questions sur les donations. — VII. Ordonnance sur les substitutions. — VIII. Traité des curés primitifs.
381 — Traité des curés primitifs. Toulouse, 1736. 4to. calf. 3.50
382 — Traité de la seigneurie féodale universelle, et du franc-allen naturel. Paris, 1767. sm. 8vo. boards. 2.—
383 **Furstenberg, G. von,** Detentio ad Caesaris auctoritatem justa etc. Trad. a. Ch. Wolfango No pl. 1674. — **Invasio** ac captivitas W. a Furstenberg in logo paci.... contra jus gentium german. Warstadt, 1674. — 2 pieces. 4to. 2.—
384 **Fürstener, C.,** De jure suprematu ac legationi principum Germaniae. No pl. 1678. sm. 8vo. calf, 3.—

385 **Gabcken, L. F.,** Grundsätze de Dorf- u. Bauernrecht . Nebst einer Vorrede v. d. Nebentheilen d. posit. Rechtsgelahrtheit von Daniel Nettelbladt. Halle, 1780. Hfcalf. 12.50

386 **Gaill, A.,** Practicarum observationum, tam ad processum judiciarium, praesertim imperialis camerae, quam causarum decisiones pertinentium ll. II. Col. Agrip. 1626. 2 vols. in 1. 4to. vellum. 6.—

387 **Gaius,** Institutiones. J. Oiselius ill. L. B. 1668. sm. 8vo. vellum. 1.50

388 — **Polenaar, B. J.,** Adnotat. ad Gai comment. III. L. B. 1876. 1.25

389 **Galganettus, P.,** De conditionibus et demonstrationib. modo, causa et poena. Ven. 1609. fol. vellum. 5.—

390 **Gargiareus, J. B.,** Consilia. Vol. I. (all publ.). Bon. 1638. fol. vellum. 7.50

391 **Garsia a Saabedra, J.,** Tractatus de donatione remuneratoria, de tacito fideicommisso, etc. Amst., J. Ravestein, 1646. sm. 8vo. vellum. 2.50

392 **Gebauer, G. Chr.,** Narratio de H. Brenkmanno de mss. Brenckmann, de suis in corpore juris civilis conatibus et laboribus. Gott. 1764. W. facs. 4to. Hfvellum. 3.—

393 **Gentilis, Sc.,** Opera omnia (juridica). Neapoli, 1763–69. 8 vols. With portraits. 4to. vellum. 40.—

394 **Genua, N.,** De scriptura privata. Ed. 3a. Adj. de verbis enunciativis. Ed. 2a. Ven. 1615. 2 vols. in 1. fol. vellum. 5.—

395 **Gerichtsordnung, Kaiser Karls des Ven peinliche,** nebst der Bamberger Halsgerichtsordnung. N. d. Ausg. von 1533 und 1507 hrsg. von R. Schmid. Jena, 1835. 2.—

396 **Gesatz** und ordenunge der loblichen und hochberümptē Freyen statt. Straszburg, 1501. Straszb. (1501). 66 ll. with woodcuts. 3.—
Facsimile after the only copy known in the Stiftsbibliothek at Einsiedeln.
Elsässische Frühdrucke, nr. 1.

397 **Gibert, J. P.,** Corpus iuris cannonici, incl. Tract. de beneficiis ecclesiast. Col. Allobr. 1735. 3 vols. W. portrait. fol. vellum and hfvellum. (Binding slightly damaged). 7.50

398 **Gierke, J.,** Die Geschichte des deutschen Deichrechts. Breslau, 1901. Vol. I (only publ.). 3.—
Untersuchungen z. dtschen Staats- und Rechtsgesch. no. 63.

399 **Giurba, M.,** Consilia seu decisiones criminales. Col. Allobr. 1645. fol. vellum. 6.—

400 **Gobius, A.,** De iure intestatae successionis. Mantuae, 1701. fol. vellum. 4.50

401 **(Godefroy, D.),** Mémoires et instructions pour servir dans les négociations et affaires concern. les droits du roy de France. Amst., A la sphère, 1665. calf. 4.50

402 **Göhrum, C. G.,** Geschichtl. Darstellung der Lehre von der Ebenbürtigkeit nach gemeinem deutschen Rechte. Tüb. 1846. 2 vols. in 1. boards. 8.50

403 **Goldschmidt, L.,** Universalgeschichte des Handelsrechts. I: Die Grundprobleme, das Altherthums, das Mittelalter, die Mittelmeerstaates, etc. Stuttg. 1891. Hfcalf. (Handb. d. Handelsrechts, 3e Aufl. I). 15.—
Original imprint. All published. Very sought after.

404 **Golinus, F.,** De procuratoribus. Acc. notae C. A. de Luca. Neap. 1683. fol. vellum. 6.—

405 **Gomezius, A.,** Commentariorum variarumque resolutionum juris civilis tomi III i: (Ultimarum solutitatum materia; contractuum; delirorum). Col. Allobr. 1622. fol. Hfcalf. 8.—

406 **Gomez de Sylva, L.,** Ad quaestionem: „Quando liceat heredi venire contra factum defuncti." Mediol. 1672. fol. vellum. (back damaged). 5.—

407 **Göppert, (H.),** Die organ. Erzeugnisse. Untersuch. a. d. röm. Sachenrecht. Halle, 1869. 2.—

408 — Einheitl. zuasmmengesetzte und Gesammt-Sachen nach röm. Recht. 1871. 1.—

409 **Gothofredus, J.,** Opera juridica minora. Lugd. Bat. 1733. W. portrait. folio. Hfcalf. 10.—

410 **Grassus, M.,** De successione. Ven. 1619. 4to. Hfvellum. 5.—

411 **Gravina, J. V.,** Originum juris civilis ll. III. Ed. 2a. Neapoli, 1713. 2 vols. 4to. vellum. 7.50

412 **Gregorius, P.,** Syntagna iuris universi atque legum pene omnium gentium praecipuarum. Francof. B. Fischerus, 1591. 3 vols. in 2. fol. Hfvellum. 12.—

413 **Grimaudet, Fr.,** Paraphrase du droict des dixmes ecclésiast. et inféodées. Paris, R. Estienne, 1571. limp vellum. 6.50

414 **Grimm, J.,** Deutsche Rechtsalterthümer. 4e verm. Ausg. d. A. Heusler und R. Hübner. Lpz. 1899. 2 vols. Hfcalf. 34.—
Last edition, original imprint.

415 **Grivelius, J.,** Decisiones senatus Dolani. G. Divione, 1731. folio. vellum. 15.—
The best edition, containing 192 decisions. The first edition (1606) contains 150 decisions only.

416 **Grosch, G.,** Markgenossenschaft und Grossgrundhersschaft im früheren Mittelalter. Berlin, 1911. 2.—
Historische Studien, H. 96.

417 **Grossus, M. A.,** De successionibus ab intestato ad interpret. consuetudinum Neapolitan· Neap. 1678. fol. vellum. 7.50

418 **Gryphiandre, J.,** De insulis tractatus. Ex ICtis polit., histor. et philolog. collectus. Francof. 1623. 4to. vellum. (paperspotted). 5.—

419 **Guerra, P.,** Il diritto d'Albinaggio e la filosofia del secolo XVIII. Firenze, 1900. (Slightly waterstained). 2.—

420 **Guiné, F.,** Traités de la representation; du double lien, et de la règle paterna paternis, materna maternis par rapport à toutes les coûtumes de France. Nouv. éd. Paris, 1773. sm. 8vo. calf. 3.50

421 **Gutierrez, J.,** Opera omnia civilia, canonica et criminalia. Col. Allobr. (Genève). 1730. 16 vols. in 5. folio. calf. 100.—
Very scarce.

422 **Guy Pape,** La jurisprudence de Guy Pape dans ses décisions. Av. notes p. N. Chorier. Lyon, 1692. 4to. veau. 15.—
First edition of the translation of the celebrated Guy de la Pape.

423 **Guyot, G. A.,** Institutes féodales ou manuel des fiefs et censures, et droits en dépendans. Paris, 1753. sm. 8vo. calf. 2.50

424 **Hahn, F. von,** Die materielle Uebereinstimmung der römischen und germanischen Rechtsprincipien. Jena, 1856. bound. 5.—

425 **Hallwachs, J. C.,** De centena illimitata s. territoriali. Francof. 1746. 4to. boards. 2.50

426 **Hane, L. van den,** Vlaems recht, dat is costumen ende wetten ghedecreteert by de graven ende gravinnen van Vlaenderen. Ghendt, 1664. fol. Hfcalf. 25.—

427 **Hartung, F.,** Deutsche Verfassungsgeschichte vom 15. Jahrh. bis zur Gegenwart. Berlin, 1914. 2.—
Grundriss der Geschichtswissenschaft, II, 4.

428 **Hasenbalg, H.,** Zur Lehre von der actio Pauliana. Berlin, 1874. 1.—

429 **Haugwitz, A. A. ab,** De regni et aulae mareschallorum nomine, origine, juribus, etc. Budissae, 1690. 4to. 5.—

430 **Hazewinkel-Suringa, D.,** Mancipatio en traditio. Bijdr. tot de kennis van de eigendomsoverdracht in het Romeinsche recht. Alphen, 1931. 2.50

431 **Hecht, F.,** Die röm. Kalendarienbücher. Heidelb. 1868. bound. 1.—

432 **Heck, Ph.,** Die Gemeinfreien der karolingischen Volksrechte. Halle, 1900. bound. 4.—
Beitr. z. Geschichte der Stände im Mittelalter. I.

433 **Heinecius, J. G.,** Opera ad univ. juris prudentiam, philosoph. et litteras humaniores pertin. Genevae, 1744–48. 8 vols. 4to. calf. 45.—
Vol. VIII contains: Praelectiones in Hug. Grotium de jure belli et pacis.

434 **Henrys, C.,** Oeuvres. 6e éd. Avec observations par Bretonnier et Terrasson. Paris, 1772. 4 vols. fol. calf. 40.—
„Les decisions de ce célèbre jurisconsulte ont été regardées comme des lois." Dupin.

435 **d'Héricourt, L.,** Oeuvres posthumes. Paris, 1759. 4 vols. 4to. boards, uncut. 20.—
I. Ses consultations canoniques et civiles. — II–IV. Memoires sur des questions de droit civil.

436 **Heringius, J.,** Tractatus singularis de molendinis eorumque jure. Francof. 1625. 4to. vellum. 10.—
At the end: **Heringius ,J.,** Mantissa, tractatui de molendinis.

437 **Hermann, E.,** Entwicklung des altdeutschen Schöffengerichts. Breslau, 1881. *Reprint.* 1.25

438 **Hermannus, I.,** Notae in Haedani postr. thesin De origine erroris. L. B. 1669. 4to. 2.50

439 **Hoetink, H. R.,** Periculum est emptoris. Beschouwingen over de gegrondheid van den aanval op de classiciteit van dezen Romeinsch-rechtelijken regel. Haarlem, 1928. 1.50

440 **Hoffmann, J. W.,** Sammlung ungedruckter und zu den Geschichten, auch Staats- Lehn- und andern Rechten des Heil. Römischen Reichs gehöriger Nachrichten, Documenten und Urkunden. Halle, 1736, 37. 2 vols. 4to. vellum. 10.—

441 **Hollander, H. v.,** Zur Lehre vom „Error" nach römischen Recht. 2e Ausg. Halle, 1908. 1.50

442 **Holtius, A. C.,** Historiae juris rom. lineamenta. Ultr. 1840. 1.50

443 — Geschied- en rechtskundige verhandelingen. Utrecht, 1851. bound. 2.50
Geschied. en overblijfselen van Pisa. — Over de Judsche wet. — Wisbysche zeeregt. — De Tabula amalfitana.

444 **Holzinger,** Die Schwurgerichte in Württemberg. Stuttg. 1849. Hfcalf. 4.—

445 **Hombergk zu Schencklengsfeld, J. Ph.,** Dissertatio juridica de ferrarum persecutione in territorio alieno, vulgo: Jagd-Folge. Giessen, 1750. 4to. calf. 4.—

446 **Hooch, N. van der,** Singularia juris. Antv. 1620. sm. 8vo. calf. 4.75

447 **Hotoman, F.,** Quaestionum illustrium liber. Paris, H. Stephanus, 1573. sm. 8vo. calf. 7.50

447*a* **Huber, U.,** Praelectionum juris civilis ll. III. Ed. 2a. Franequerae, L. Strick, 1700–01. 3 vols. W. portrait. 4to. vellum. 15.—

448 — — The same. Acc. C. Thomsori additiones et L. Menckenii remissiones ad jus saxonicum. Ed. J. Le Plat. Lovanii, 1766. 3 vols. 4to. calf. 12.—

449 — Eunomia Romana s. censura censurae juris Justin. Ed. Z. Huber. Franeq., L. Strickius, 1700. 4to. vellum. 7.50

450 — De jure civitatis. Ed. 4a. Franequerae, B. Wibranda, 1708. 4to. calf. (Binding slightly damaged). 10.—

451 **Hüllmann, K. D.,** Staedtewesen des Mittelalters. Bonn, 1826–29. 4 vols. Hfcalf. 24.—
I. Kunstfleis und Handel. — II. Grundverfassung. — III. Gemeinheitsverfassung. — IV. Bürgerleben.

452 — Geschichte der Domainen-Benutzung in Deutschland. Frankf. 1807. 5.—

453 — Staedtewesen des Mittelalters. Bonn, 1826–29. 4 vols. Hfcalf. 18.—

454 — Römische Grundverfassung. Bonn, 1832. Hfcalf. 5.—

455 — Geschichte des Ursprungs der deutschen Fürstenwürde. Bonn, 1842. boards. 5.—

456 **Hunnius, H. U.,** Resolut. iuris civilis. Francof. 1670. 4to. vellum. 3.—

457 **Hunt, Th.,** Defence of the charter and municip. rights of London and of other municip. cities etc. of England. London, (ab. 1680). 4to. 2.50

458 **Ickstadt, J. A. von,** Gründliche Abhandlungen von den Jagdrechten. Mit Anhang von den neuesten mehrenteils ungedruckten Jagdordnungen. Nebst Entwurf von einer Waldordnung. Nürnberg, 1749. 4to. calf. 5.—

459 **Ihering, R.,** Entwicklungsgeschichte des römischen Rechts. Einleitung: Verfassung des römischen Hauses. A. d. Nachlass hrsg. v. Victor Ehrenberg. Lpz. 1894. 3.50

460 **Jacquet,** Traité des fiefs. Paris, 1762. sm. 8vo. calf. 4.—

461 — Traité des justices de seigneur, et des droits en dépendants. Lyon, 1764. 4to. calf. 6.—

462 **Jarcke, C. E.,** Versuch einer Darstellung der censorischen Strafrechts der Römer. Bonn, 1824. Hfcalf. 2.—

463 **Jenichen, G. A.,** Thesaurus juris feudalis. Francof. 1750–54. 3 vols. 4to. vellum. 15.—

464 **Joüon des Longrais, F.,** La conception anglaise de la saisine du 12e au 14e siècle. Paris, 1925. 7.50
Etudes des droits anglais. I.

465 **(Jousse, D.),** Nouveau commentaire sur les ordonnances du mois d'août 1669, et mars 1673, ensemble sur l'édit de 1673 touchant les épices. Nouv. éd. Paris, 1777. sm. 8vo. calf. 3.—

466 — Traité de la justice criminelle de France. Paris, 1771. 4 vols. 4to. calf. 12.—

467 **Jovius, A.,** De solemnitatibus in contractibus minorum. Parmae, 1694. fol. vellum 6.—

468 **Jungius, J. H.,** De jure salinarum tum veteri tum hodierno. Acc. C. Sagittarii de originibus.... sulciae Luneburgensis.... nec non Sylloge documentorum plur. indeit. pro salina Lunebergensi. Gott. 1743. W. 2 pl. 4to. vellum. 10.—
Cap. II, 88 pp.: De salinarum jure apud Germanos.

469 **Juris orientalis** ll. III. ab E. Bonefidio digesti, notis illustr. Gr. et Lat. (Paris), H. Stephanus, 1573. 3 parts in 1 vol. calf. (binding damaged). 15.—
I. Constitut. imperat. ab Heraclio ad Michaelem Palaeologum. — II. Sanctiones patriarcharum, Constantinop. a Johanne Chrysotomo ad Caesarem Athanasium. — III. Responsa, epistola et sententiae aliorum patriarcharum.

470 **Jurisprudentia** vetus ante-Justinianea. Ed. A. Schultingius. Lpz. 1737. 4to. calf. 4.—

471 **Jurisprudentia vetus.** Draconis et Solonis leges, P. Prateio collect. et interpr. Lugd., G. Rovillius, 1559. — **Floccus, A. D.,** De potestatibus Romanorum. Antv., G. Sylvius, 1561. — 2 vols. in 1. 8.50

472 **Juspublicum,** (S. Imperii Romani), hoc est de Romani imperatoris electione, vicaria imperii administratione, principum electorum sessione, successione, tutela, privilegiis, etc. Francof. 1620. 2 vols. in 1. 4to. vellum. 8.50

473 **ustinianus.** — CORPUS JURIS: DIGESTUM NOVUM. Roma, S. Marcus (= Vitus Puecher), 1476. 412 ll. fol. oaken boards, covered with stamped leather. 2400.—

Hain, nr. 9580. Gesamtkatalog, nr. 7701. Extremely scarce, no copy in U.S.A. according to Gesamtkatalog.

An exceptionally fine, clean and tall copy (some leaves uncut) of the famous **editio princeps.** The text begins with a beautiful miniature and 13 initials exquisitely coloured and heightened with gold in the best italian style. The contemporary binding has slightly suffered.

474 — **Corpus juris civilis** cum glossis. Geneva, 1625. 6 vols. fol. vellum, with ties. 150.—

I. Digestum vetus. — II. Infortiatum pandectarum. — III. Digestum novum pandectarum. — IV. Codicis sacratissimi ll. XII. — V. Volumen legum parvum. — VI. Index.

475 — **Corpus iuris civilis.** C. notis D. Gothofredi et S. van Leeuwen. Amst., D. Elsevier, 1663. 2 vols. folio. calf, backs red morocco gilt. 35.—

Willems, no. 1299. The celebrated Elsevier-edition.

476 — — The same. Ed. nova Amst., Elsevier, 1664. 2 vols. in 1. W. engraved titlepage. 8vo. calf. 12.50

Willems, no. 1323.

477 — — The same. Ed. nova. Amst., Blaeu, 1700. W. engraved titlepage. Russia. 10.—

478 — — The same. Ed. nova. adaucta. Colon. 1759. 2 vols. in 1. 4to. calf. 3.—

479 — — Rec. A. et M. Kriegelii, A. Herrmann etc. Editio stereotypa. Lips. 1858. 3 vols. Hfcalf. 6.—

480 — **Digestorum** seu pandectarum ll. L. Antv., Chr. Plantin, 1575. 2 vols. fol. calf. 15.—

481 — — The same. Ed. Th. Mommsen. Berlin, 1866. 4to. 4.—

482 — **Decisiones** quae a 2° liber Codicis usque ad eum diffusae sunt. Per P. F. Linglois. Antw. 1622. fol. vellum. 5.—

483 — **Andler, F. F.,** Medulla juris Justinianei. Herbipoli, 1662. W. engraved titlepage and portrait. sm. 8vo. vellum. 2.50

484 — **Assen, C. J. van,** Lineamenta extrema juris privati Justinianei sec. text. institt. Leiden, 1856. 1.50

485 — **Bolognetti, J.,** Super prima et secunda parte Digesti veteris. Repetitiones copiosissima earum legum quae in studiis Italiae magis frequentantur. Napoli, R. de Amata, 1555. 2 parts in 1 vol. folio. oaken boards, back pigskin. 25.—

486 — **Borcholten, J.,** Commentaria in Institutionem juris civilis ll. IV. Lovanii, 1646. 4to. calf. 6.—

487 — **Boutaric, F. de,** Les Institutes de l'empereur Justinien, conferées avec le droit françois. Toulouse, 1740. 4to. calf. 4.—

488 — **Brunnemann, J.,** Commentarius in Pandectas. Francof. 1670. W. front. folio. vellum. 15.—

First edition of the celebrated commentaries.

489 — — The same. Comment. in Pandectas. Recogn. S. Strykius. Ed. 5a. Wittenb. 1701. W. front. fol. vellum. 5.—

490 — — Commentarius in codicem Justinianeum. Lips. 1717. W. frontisp. folio. vellum. 12.—

491 — **Cujacius, J.,** Novellarum Justin. expositio. — **De feudis** ll. V, quorum primus est G. Nigri, secundus et tertius O. de Orto, etc. Auct. en emend. J. Cujacius. — Col. Agrip., J. Gymnicus, 1592, 88. In 1 vol. vellum. 7.50

492 — **Drosaeus, J.,** Juris universi Justinianea methodus. Paris., M. Dupuy, 1545. sm. 8vo. calf. (rebacked). 4.—

The prelim. ll. 2–3 are missing.

493 — **Dupleix, S.,** In Institut. Justin. comment. — **Id.,** Axiomata sententiae et regulae juris. — Paris, 1635. 2 vols. in 1. calf. 3.—

494 — **Grandus, G.,** Epistola de Pandectis ad Jos. Averanium. Ed. alt. App. Veterum Monumentorum (715–1343) locupl. Flor. 1727. 4to. vellum. 5.—

Bound up with: **V. Valsechius,** Epistola de veteribus Pisanae civitatis constitutis ad G. Grandi.

495 — **Hahn, H.,** Observata ad M. Wesenbecii in L. ll. Digestorum commentarios. Helmstad, 1668. 2 vols. in 1. W. front. fol. vellum. 5.—

496 — — The same. Ed. 3a. Col. Agripp. 1675. 2 vols. in 1. fol. vellum. (Binding damaged) 5.—

497 — **Heineccius, J. G.,** Antiquit. Roman. jurisprudentiam ill. syntagma. Cast. et observ. auxit Ch. G. Haubold et Ch. F. Mühlenbruch. Francof. 1841. bound. 2.50

498 — — Recitat. in elementa juris civilis sec. ord. Institut. Ed. P. de Ryckere. Gand. 1818. 1.50

499 — **Hopp, J.,** Comment. succ. ad Institut. Justin. Francof. 1731. W. portrait. 4to. vellum. 4.50
500 — **Hotoman (Hotman), F.,** Commentarius in IV ll. Institutionum juris civilis. Lugduni, A. Gryphius, 1567. fol. limp vellum. 12.—
501 — **Huber, U.,** Digressiones Justinianeae. Ed. 3a ex rec. Z. Huber. Franeker, J. Horreus, 1696. 4to. vellum. 7.50
502 — **Jansma v. d. Ploeg, G. P.,** Het Romeinsche regt. n. aanleid. der Instit. 's-Grav. 1851. bound. 1.50
503 — **Kleinschrod, G. F. E.,** Über L. 27 dig. de rebus creditis, m. bes. Bezieh. auf Darlehen an Gemeinden. Heidelb. 1851. 1.75
504 — **Kling, M.,** In Institutionum juris Justiniani enarrationes. Lugd., G. Rovillius, 1557. Hfcalf. (Waterstained). 6.—
505 — **Leyser, A. à,** Meditationes ad Pandectas. Ed. absolv., opusc. nonnulla et indices adj. G. A. Jenichem. Ed. 3a. Lps. 1741–62. 11 vols. 4to. Hfcalf. 15.—
In 1774 a twelfth volume was published, written by Höpfner.
506 — **Ludewig, J. P.,** Vita Justin. Magni atque Theodorae; Augustorum nec non Triboniani jurisprudentiae Justin. proscenium. Hal. 1731. W. front., map and 7 pl. 4to. calf. 2.50
507 — **Mandowsky, O.,** Hundert Stellen a. d. Corpus juris. Breslau, 1885. 1.—
508 — **Matthaeus, A.,** Commentarius ad Institutiones Justiniani. Ultraj. P. Elzevir, 1672. 4to. vellum. 6.—
509 — **Merillius, E.,** Institut. imperial. comment. princip. ll. IV. Ed. C. Mengin. C. praef. C. H. Trotz. Ultr., J. Broedelet, 1739. 4to. Hfcalf. 3.—
510 — — [Opera]. Observat. ll. VIII. Notae philol. in passionem Christi. Expos. in 4 decisiones Justiani, Variantium ex Cujaco ll. III. etc. Neapoli, 1720. 2 vols. in 1. 4to. vellum. 5.—
511 — **Mornacius, A.,** Observatt. in 50 ll. Pandedtarum ,in ll. Codicis. Paris. 1721. 4 vols. in 2. folio. vellum. 20.—
512 — **Muelen, W. van der,** Exercitatt. in titul. Digest. de justitia et jure et historiam Pomponii de origine juris. Ultr., G. vande Water, 1723. 4to. vellum. 5.—
513 — **Mynsingerus a Frundeck, J.,** Ad IV ll. Institut. iuris civilis. Ven. 1612. fol. vellum. (binding damaged). 3.50
514 — **Nicasius de Voerda, D.,** Institut. Imp. ll. IV. Francof., I. Wechel., 1583. sm. 8vo. pigskin. (Titlepage short and the binding is damaged). 4.50
515 — **Oinotomus, J.,** In IV Institut. Justin. ll. comment. Ven. 1720. fol. vellum. 5.—
516 — **Pacius à Beriga, J.,** Institut. imperial. analysis, et selecta. Lugd. 1621. sm. 8vo. Hfcalf. 2.—.
517 — **Perezius, A.,** Praelectiones in XII ll. codicis Justiniani. Amst., L et D. Elzevir, 1661. 2 vols. in 1. 4to. veau. 7.50
Willems, no. 1273.
518 — — The same. Praelectiones in XII ll. codicis Justiniani. Amst., D. Elsevir, 1671. 2 vols. 4to. calf. 7.50
Willems, no. 1457.
519 — — Institutiones Imper. erotematibus distinctae. Ed. 7a. Amst., L. Elzevir, 1652. 12mo. calf. (Mod. binding). 7.50
520 — **Picardus, J. C.,** Annotatt. ad Institut., Pandectas et Codicem Justin. Lugd., J. Tornaesius, 1558. 4to. vellum. 5.—
521 — **Pothier, R. J.,** Pandectes de Justinien, mises dans un nouvel ordre etc. Trad. par de Bréard-Neuville. (Latin and french text). Paris, 1818–23. 24 vols. W. portrait. Hfcalf. 25.—
522 — **Reverdy, H.,** Les donations dans la législation de Justinien, et dans les pays de droit écrit. Poitiers, 1897. 4.—
523 — **Riminaldus, H.,** In aliquot Institut. imperial. titulos comment. Ven., J. B. Somaschus, 1583. W. portrait. fol. Hfvellum. 4.—
524 — **Ripa, J. F. à,** Commentaria in primam et secundam infortiati partem Joan. Nicolai Arelatani cura. Commentaria in utranque digesti novi partem. Interpretationes in primam decretalium. Commentaria una cum summariis in repetitiones rub. sequentium. Repetitio rubricae de judiciis. De causa posses. et proprie. De restitut. spoliatio. Tractatus de peste. Responsa in quinque libros Decretalium. Lugduni, Blasius Guido, 1554. 2 vols. folio. oaken boards, back pressed pigskin. 40.—
525 — **Ruggieri, O.,** De obligationibus. Praelectiones ad Pandectas. Romae, 1872. 1.50

526 — **Sande, J. à.,** Ad titul. Digest. de diversis regulis juris antiqui comment. Leov., J. Jansonius, 1647. 4to. vellum. 2.50

527 — **Schneidewin, J.,** In IV Institutt. imperial. Justin. ll. comment. A. M. Wesenbecio, P. Brederodio, D. Gothofredo, rec. Argent. 1652. 4to. calf. 6.—

528 — **Schulting, A.,** Thesium controversarum juxta seriem Digestorum decades C. Lugd. Bat., C. de Pecker, 1762. sm. 8vo. Hfcalf. 4.—

529 — **Sutro, S.,** Leerboek der Instituten. Tiel, 1872–83. 3 vols. cloth. 2.50

530 — **Theophilus,** Paraphrasis Graeca institut.t caesarearum. Ed. G. O. Reitz. Acc. Just. institutt. Recens. E. Schrader. Amst. 1860. 2.—

531 — **Vinnius, A.,** In IV ll. Institut. comment. Ed. 4a. Amst., D. Elsevier, 1665. 4to. vellum. 2.50

Willems, no. 1367.

532 — — The same. Recens. J. G. Heineccius. Acc. quaestiones juris selectae. Lugd. 1755. 4to. vellum. 5.—

533 — — The same. Ven. 1761. 2 vols. 4to. 3.—

534 — **Voet, J.,** Commentarius ad Pandectas. Hag. Com., A. de Hondt, 1707. 2 vols. fol. vellum. 15.—

535 — — The same. Hag. Com. 1716. 2 vols. fol. calf. (binding damaged). 15.—

536 — — The same. Colon. Allobr. 1778. 2 vols. in 1. folio. vellum, with the coats of arms of Arnhem. 25.—

Very fine and clean copy.

537 — **Voet, P.,** In IV ll. Institut. imperialium commentarius. Gorinchem, P. Vink, 1668. 2 vols. in 1. 4to. vellum. 7.50

538 — **Wesenbecius, M.,** In codicem Justiniani comment., vetus renovatus. Rec. C. Brederodius. Basil., E. Episcopius, 1590. Vol. II (only). fol. stamped leather. 6.—

Interleaved, with numerous annotations.
At the end somewhat waterstained.

539 — — In Pandectas et Cod. Just. ll. c. notis R. Bachovii. Col. Agr. 1650. — **Id.,** Perioche feudalis c. notis H. Hermes. Ibid. 1651. — **J. Schneidewinus,** In IV Inst. Justin. comment. A. M. Wesenbecio, P. Brederodio, e.a., recogn. Argent., Chr. ab Heyden, 1652– — 3 vols. in 1. 4to. vellum. 7.50

540 — **Zoesius, H.,** Commentarius ad Digestorum seu Pandectarum juris civilis ll. L. Ed. 4a. Lovanii, 1718. W. portrait. fol. vellum. 10.—

541 **Justis, V. de,** De dispensationibus matrimonialibus. Luca, 1726. 2 vols. in 1. fol. vellum. 7.50

542 **Kamphuisen, P. W.,** Gewoonterecht. 's-Grav. 1935. 3.—

West-Europa tot den tijd der Republiek. — Tot het einde der Republiek. — De grondslag voor het gewoonterecht. — Conventions. — Gewoonte in het huidige staatsrecht. — etc.

543 **Keller, F. L. von,** Der römische Civilprocess und die Actionen. 5e Ausg. Bearb. von A. Wach. Lpz. 1876. Hfcalf. 6.—

544 **Keutgen, F.,** Der deutsche Staat des Mittelalters. Jena, 1918. 2.50

545 **Keyserrecht, Das.** N. d. Hs. von 1372 in Vergleichung mit andern Hss. und mit erläut. Anmerk. hrsg. von H. E. Endemann. Cassel, 1846. boards. 10.—

Very scarce.

546 **Kinschot, H.,** Responsa s. consilia juris. It. de rescriptis gratiae a.... senatu Brabantiae.... solitis, tractatus VII. Lov. 1633. 2 vols. in 1. fol. vellum. 6.50

547 — — The same. Ed. emend. Brux. 1653. 2 vols. in 1. folio. calf. 8.50

548 **Kluber, J. L.,** Wichtige Urkunden für den Rechtszustand der deutschen Nation. Erläutert von C. Welcker. Mannheim, 1845. 5.—

549 **Knipschildt, Ph.,** De fideicommissis familiarum nobilium, sive de bonis, quae pro familiarum nobilium conservatione constituuntur. Von Stammgütern. Ulm, 1661. W. front. and portrait. 4to. vellum. 30.—

Original edition of this excellent work.

550 — Informatio de obligatione dominierga vasallum, d.i.: Kurtzer Bericht was ein Lehenherr seinen Lehenmann zu thun schuldig. Ulm, 1656. — **Fritsch, A.,** De gratia principis ergo ministrum. Jena, 1664. — **Sparr, J. C. à,** Assertiones de beneficiis ecclesiasticis. Aug. Trev. 1687. — In 1 vol. sm. 8vo. vellum. 6.—

551 **Kooiman, C. L.,** Fragmenta juris quiritum 1913. Amst. 1914. W. annotations in ms. 2.50

552 **Kriminalrecht, Das Nürnberger,** nach Rats-Urkunden erläutert von H. Knapp. Berlin, 1896. boards. 3.—

553 **Krones, F. von,** Verfassung und Verwaltung der Mark und des Herzogthums Steier von ihrer Anfängen b. z. Herrschaft der Habsburger. Graz, 1897. Hfcalf. 4.50
Forschungen z. Verfass. und Verwalt. gesch. der Steiermark. I.

554 **Krul, J. G.,** De regali monetarum jure. Jena, 1667. 4to. (slightly waterstained). 2.50

555 **Labberton, D. van Hinloopen,** De middeleeuwsche oorsprong en geschiedenis van het Engelsche parlementaire stelsel. Magna Carta libertatum en Witena-Gemot. 's-Grav. 1931. 3.60

556 **Lacuisine, de,** Le parlement de Bourgogne depuis son origine jusqu'à sa chute; précédé d'un discours du Dijon et ses institutions. Dyon, 1857. 2 vols. W. portrait. Hfcalf. 12.—

557 **Laferrière, F.,** Histoire de droit français précédée d'une introduction sur le droit civil de Rome. Paris, 1852–58. 6 vols. Hfcalf. 24.—
Scarce.

558 **(La Garde, F. de Paul),** Traité historique des droits du souverain en France, et principalement des droits utilés et domaniaux. Paris, 1767. 2 vols. 4to. calf. 7.50

559 **Lagrèze, G. B. de,** Histoire du droit dans les Pyrénées (comté de Bigorre). Paris, 1867. 8.—

560 **Lalli, C.,** De reo contumace disceptat. criminales. Roma, 1748. fol. Hfvellum. 4.50

561 **Lambertinus, C.,** De iure patronatus. Ven. 1572. 3 vols. in 1. fol. vellum. 9.—

562 **Lamberts Hurrelbrinck, P. H. L.,** De wetgeving der twaalf tafelen in het licht van den Romeinschen godsdienst. 's-Grav. 1918. 1.50

563 **Lancelottus, J. P.,** Institutiones juris canonici. Lovan., H. Wellaeus, 1578. calf. (Binding damaged, clasps gone). 7.50

564 — — The same. Institutiones juris canonici. Paris, 1685. 2 vols. sm. 8vo. calf. (rebacked). 4.50

565 **Landes-Ordnungen, Lieffländische,** nebst darzu gehörigen Placaten und Stadgen. Riga, 1707. 4to. vellum. 30.—

566 **Landgüterordnung, Die,** für die Provinz Westfalen vom 30. April 1882. Hrsg. von M. Hartmann. Paderborn, 1882. — **Funke, G. L. W.,** Die heillosen Folgen der Bodenzersplitterung und deren Gefahren für ganz Europa. Gött. 1854. — **Riepenhausen-Orangen K. von,** Gesicherte Familienheimstätten für alle Stände im Deutschen Reich. Lpz. 1891. — **Heimstättenrecht** ein Recht für Jedermann. Berlin, 1891. — **Baernreither,** Stammgüter System und Auerbenrecht in Deutschland. Wien, 1882. — **Pfaff, L.,** und **F. Hofmann,** Zur Geschichte der Fideicommisse. Wien, 1884. — **Hager, P.,** Familienfideikommisse. Jena, 1897. — etc. Tog. 8 pieces in 1 vol. bound. 10.—

567 **Land Recht, Ernewert gemein,** des Hertzogthumsb Württemberg. Stuttg. 1626. sm. fol. boards. 18.—

568 **Landrecht, Das württembergische** vom 1. Juni 1610. Neue Ausg. besorgt von C. H. Riecke. Stuttg. 1842. boards. 4.50

569 **Landrecht,** der Graffschaft Hohenlohe. Mit denen benöthigten Marginalen und Registern. Oehringen, 1738. fol. boards. 10.—

570 **Landrecht, Das badische,** nebts Handelsgesetzen. Karlsruhe, 1840. 1.50

571 **Lands-Bräuche, Die gemeine,** des Hertzogthums Lutzenberg und Graffschaft Chiny. Lutzenburg (1709). 5 pieces in 1 vol. sm. 8vo. calf. (Librarystamp on titlepage). 5.—

572 **Landts Ordnungen, Gemeine,** desz Hertzogthumbs Würtemberg, denen.... fürstliche General Auszschreiben,.... als Novellae constitutiones zuend angehenckt. Stuttg. 1621. sm. fol. boards. 12.—

573 **Lange,** La nouvelle pratique civile criminelle et beneficiale, ou le nouveau praticien français. Cologne, 1731. 4to. calf. 6.—

574 **Lange, P. A. de,** De fragmentis Alfeni Vari digestorum a Paulo epitomatorum. Amst. 1835. 1.25

575 **Lapi de Castellhovo,** Tractatus allegationum.... omnibus jurisprudentiae studiosis utilissimus. Lugduni, (J. Junta), 1537. stamped pigskin. 36.—
Bound up with: **Matthaeus de Afflictis,** De jure prothomiseos. Lugduni, J. Giuncti, 1539. (At the end): Impressum per Benedictum Bonyn.

576 **Lappe, J.,** Die Wüstungen der Provinz Westfalen. Einleitung: Die Rechtsgeschichte der wüsten Marken. Münster, 1916. 1.25
Veröffentl. d. histor. Kommission f. die Prov. Westfalen.

577 **Larsen, J. E.,** Retshistorikse Afhandlinger og Foredrag. Yderligere Undersögelse over Christian II's love. — Danske Provindsiallovbögers Historie. — Retshistor. Ammeldelser. Kjöbenh. 1861. Hfcalf. 6.50

578 **Laspeyres, E. A.,** Ueber die Entstehung und älteste Bearbeitung der libri feudorum. Berlin, 1830. boards. 12.—
Very scarce.

579 **Le Bret, C.,** Oeuvres. Nouv. éd. Rouen, 1689. fol. calf. 12.—
Cont.: Ses décisions sur le domaine et autres choses publiques; ses playdoyers avec les arrêts, etc.

580 **Le Brun, D.,** Traité de la communauté entre mari et femme, avec un traité des communautés au sociétés tacites. Nouv. éd. Paris, 1754. fol. calf. 15.—

581 — Traité des successions. Avec de nouvelles décisions etc. par F. B. Espiard de Siaux. Nouv. éd. Paris, 1775. fol. calf. 15.—
The best edition.

582 **Leeuwen, S. van,** De origine et progressu jur. civ. Rom. authores et fragmenta vet. jurisconsult. C. not. A. Vinnii et var. L. B., A. Doude, C. Driehuysen, 1671. W. front. sm. 8vo.vellum. 2.50

583 — Censura forensis theoret. practica i.e. totius juris civ. method. coll. Ed. 3a altera parte auctior. Amst. 1685. 2 vols. in 1. fol. vellum. 7.50

584 — — The same. Amst. 1688. 2 vols. in 1. fol. vellum. 7.50

585 **Le Febure, L. Ch.,** Traité des fiefs et de leur origine. Paris, 1662. fol. vellum. 7.50

586 **Lefebure de la Bellande,** Traité général des droits d'aides. Paris, 1760. 4to. calf. 7.50

587 **Leges antiquae Barbarorum.** C. not. et glossar. Coll. P. Canciani. Acc. formularum fascic. et sel. constitutiones medii aevi. Venetiis, 1781–92. 5 vols. fol. Hfcalf. 165.—
Borchard, Guide to the law liter. of Germany: „A very good edition of these so-called barbarian laws is that by Canciani".
This collection of barbarian laws is much sought after and very scarce.

588 **Leges Longobardorum** seu capitulare.... Carolimagni imperatoris Novelle Constitutones Justinia c. annot. Nic. Boherii. (Lyon, Symon Vincent, 1512). 4to. Hfvellum. (Mod. binding). 45.—

589 **Leges Visigothorum** antiquiores (ex monumentis German. histor.). ed. K. Zeumer. Hann. 1894. 7.50
Out of print.

590 **Leges** novellae imperatorum Theodosii Jr. et Valentiniani III ac Lex Romana s. responsum Papisani. C. praefat. et notis Joh. Christ. Amadutii. Roma, 1767. W. facs. fol. Hfvellum. 5.—

591 **Le Grand. — Remarques** sur le commentaire de Me. L. le Grand, sur la coutume de Troyes, à l'usage des Pays-Bas Autrichiens et princip. du duché de Brabant. Brux. 1777. 1re partie (all published?). fol. calf. 5.—

592 **Leis extravagantes,** college relat. p. Duarte Nunez do Lião p. mandado do rei D. Sebastião (c. 1480–1570). Coimbra, 1796. 4to. calf. (Name cut out from titlepage). 15.—

593 **Leiserus, G. C.,** Jus georgicum, s. tract. de praediis. Lps. 1698. W. 4 pl. fol. calf. 5.—

594 — — The same. Ed. 2a. Lps. 1713. W. front. fol. vellum. 5.—

595 — — The same. Ed. 3a. Lps. 1741. W. front. fol. vellum. 5.—

596 **Leist, B. W.,** Dogmat. Analyse römischer Rechtsinstitute. Jena, 1854. 1.—

597 — Graeco-italische Rechtsgeschichte. Jena, 1884. Hfcalf. 18.—

598 **Le Merre, P.,** Justific. des usages de France sur les mariages des enfans faits sans le consentement. Paris, 1687. calf. 3.50

599 **Le Moy, A.,** Le parlement de Bretagne et le pouvoir royal au 18e siècle. Angers, 1909. 7.50

600 **Leo, M. A.,** Praeparatorium iudiciorum tam civilium quam criminalium. 2 vols. — **J. Tanaglius,** Urbis et orbis supremi tribunalis monumenta s. de Sacro rotae Rom. auditoria, etc. — Liburni, 1654, 51. 3 vols. in 1. fol. vellum. 6.—

601 **Leonhard, R.,** Der Irrthum bei nichtigen Verträgen n. römischen Rechte. Berlin, 1882, 83. 2 vols. W. a few. annotat. 1.75

602 — Roms Vergangenheit und Deutschlands Recht. Lpz. 1889. 1.50

603 **Leoninus, E.,** Emendationum ll. VII. In quibus pleraeque utilissimaemateriae pertractantur. Arnhem, I. Iansonius, 1710. 4to. vellum. 4.50

604 **Leotardus, H.,** De usuris et contractibus usurariis coërcendis. Ed. 3a corr. et emend. Lugd. 1602. fol. vellum.

605 — — The same. Ed. 4a. Lugd. 1682. fol. vellum. 4.—

606 — — The same. Brixiae, 1701. fol. Hfvellum. (back damaged). 3.75

607 **Lesrat, G. de,** Arrests notables, donnez en lacour de parlement de Bretagne, et prononcez en Robbe rouge. Paris, 1588. limp vellum. 5.—

608 **Lewis, W.,** Das Recht des Familienfideicommisses. Berlin, 1868. — **Schulze, H. J. F.,** Das Recht der Erstgebort in den deutschen Fürstenhäusern und seine Bedeutung für die deutsche Staatsentwicklung. Lpz. 1851. — In 1 vol. bound. 20.—
The first work is extremely scarce.

609 **Lex Romana** Visigothorum. Instr. G. Haenel. Lps. 1849. royal 4to. 25.—
Out of print and much sougth after.

610 **Lex Salica.** The ten texts with the glosses and the lex emend., ed. by J. H. Hessels, with notes on the Frankish words by H. Kern. London, 1880. 4to. cloth. 60.—
The best edition of the Lex Salica.
Very scarce.

611 **Leyes** ordenāças prematicas y declaraciones delas ordenancas antiguas q̄ hablan del obrage d'las lanas y paños. Sevilla, A. de Olmedo, 1538. 8 ll. fol. 100.—
Laws and ordonnances concerning wool and cloth, promulgated by Charles V. Very scarce.

612 **Lezana, J. B. de,** Consulta varia theol., jurid. et regul. circa controversias. Ven. 1651. fol. vellum. 3.50

613 **Libro** de las leyes, privilegios y provisiones reales del Conceio de la mesta general, etc. Madrid, 1681. fol. (Binding missing). 12.50

614 **(Linguet, S. N .H.),** Théorie des lois civiles, ou principes fondamentaux de la Société. Londres (Paris), 1767. 2 vols. sm. 8vo. calf. 30.—
Original edition of the principal work of Linguet.
„Cet ouvrage remarquable rejoint les théories socialistes modernes dans leurs critiques des institutions."

615 **Littleton, Th.,** Anciennes loix des François, conservées dans les coutumes angloises. (Trad.) av. observat. histor. et critiques p. Houard. Rouen, 1779. 2 vols. 4to. calf. 30.—
This work is a translation of the famous „Tenures" of Littleton, originally written in old French and appeared for the first time about 1480. It was very valuable. Brunet calls it an old and valuable monument of English law. See: Dictionary of national biography, vol. XI.
Vol. I contains the laws in Latin with French translation opposite, with remarks; vol. II contains for the greater part essays and pieces of evidence. The same edition as that of 1766, except the title.
Vol. II has suffered from water.

616 **Livre, Le,** des droiz et des commandemens d'office de justice. Publ. d'après le ms. inéd. de la bibliothèque de l'Arsenal p. C.-J. Beautemps-Beaupré. Paris, 1865. Vol. II. 2.—
2d vol. of a reprint of a ms. of 1424. „C'est un recueil de la jurisprudence des cours du Poitou dans la seconde moitié du 14e siècle."

617 **Loccenius, J.,** Sueciae regni leges provinciales, a Carolo IX anno 1608 publ. In Lat. trad et notis illustr. — **Id.,** Sueciae regni leges civiles, sec. Gustavi Adolphi mandatum publ. a. 1618. In Lat. trad. et notis illustr. Acc. regulae juris Suegothici. — Holmiae, 1672. In 1 vol. fol. Hfcalf. 24.—

618 **Lochner, J. M. F.,** Otia d.i. verschied. zur Jurispr. und Litteratur gehör. Materien. Nebst Schwarzens Vom Ursprung der Landes Hoheit teutscher Fürsten. Nürnb. 1751. sm. 8vo. calf. 3.75
Von dem iure guardiae. — Von der insinuatione donationis. — Von mündl. Testamenten — Ad leg. Rhod. de iactu. — etc.

619 **Löher, F.,** Fürsten und Städte zur Zeit der Hohenstaufen. Halle, 1846. 1.—

620 **Loi** de Vestrogothie (Codex antiquior). Trad. et annot. p. L. Beauchet. Paris, 1889. *Reprint.* 4.—

621 **Loovens, J. E.,** Practycke, stiel ende maniere van procederen in den Raede van Brabant. Brussel, 1745. 3 vols. fol. calf. 15.—

622 **Louët, G.,** Recueil de plusieurs notables arrests du parlement de Paris. Nouv. éd. par J. Brodeau. Paris, 1693. 2 vols. fol. calf. 18.—

623 **Louvrex, G. de,** Recueil cont. les edits et reglements faits pour le païs de Liège et comté de Looz....; les concordats et traitez faits avec les puissances voisines. Nouv. éd. augm. p. B. Hodin. Liège, (1749–1752). 4 vols. fol. calf. 20.—

624 **Loiseau, Ch.,** Des cas ou un pupille romain a plusieurs tuteurs. Du conflit des lois françaises et étrangères en matière de tutelle des mineurs. Lons-le-Saunier. 1885. 5.—

625 **Loix,** chartes etc. du chef-lieu de la ville de Mons. Et des villes et villages y resortissans, av. decrets en dépendans, et mesures des terres et bois. Mons, 1795. sm. 8vo. calf. 4.—

626 **Lonqueval, J. N. J. de,** Exercitatio de jure puniendi in statu naturali. Prague, 1760. 4to. calf. 7.50

627 **Lopez Madera, G.,** Animadvers. iur. civ. Col. Agr., J. Gymnicus, 1594. sm. 8vo. calf. 4.50

628 **Lopez de Segovia, J.,** De la confederacion de principes y de la guerra y de los guerreros. Facsimilé del original Latino. Trad. de F. A. Moreno. Madrid, 1931. 3.75

Facsimile reprint, with spanish translation of these two tracts of the 15th century: De confederatione principium, et: De bells et bellatoribus.

Publ. de la Asociacion Francisco de Vitoria.

629 **Loyseau, Ch.,** Oeuvres, contenant les cinq livres du droit des offices, les traitez des seigneuries, des ordres, etc. Nouv. éd. augm. Paris, 1678. fol. calf. 25.—

630 **Luca, B. de,** De credito, et debito, creditore et debitore. Romae, 1671. fol. vellum. 3.—

Theatri veritatis et justitiae. VII.

631 **Lucius Veron.,** De successione in jura ditionesq. Juliae, Cliviae, Montium, Marchiae et Ravensbergae, ... diss. etc. c. succ. deduct. pro Domo Solisbacensi, c. Mantissa. Mannh. 1732. 2 vols. in 1. fol. boards. 4.50

632 **Ludewig, J. P. de,** De jure clientelari Germanorum in feudis et coloniis. Ed. 2a. Halae, 1737. 4to. Hfcalf. 2.50

633 **Ludolf, G. M. de,** De introductione juris primogeniturae. C. append. Jena, 1733. fol. vellum. 7.50

Appendix II: Familia ducalis Saxonica lineae Ernestinae. — III. Familia Guelfica. — IV: Familia ducalis Mechlenburgica. — etc.

634 **Lünig, J. Chr.,** Das Teutsche Reichs-Archiv. Lpz. 1710–22. 24 stout vols. fol. vellum. 725.—

Very fine complete set of this very important and valuable work. See „Allgem. deutsche Biographie".

635 — Codex Germaniae diplomaticus, worinnen viele.... zur Illustration der Teutschen Reichshistorie und Jurispublici, höchstnöthige Documenta enthalten sind. Franckf. 1732, 33. 2 vol. fol. vellum. 25.—

This work forms for the greater part a supplement to Lünig's Das Teutsche Reichs-Archiv. Fine copy.

636 — Grundfeste Europäischer Potenzen Gerechtsame, worinn durch auserlesene Deductiones, Informationes, Repraesentationes etc. dargethan wird wie es sowohl um der R. Kais. Maj. als auch Chur-Fürsten etc. des heil. Röm. Reichs, ingl. auswärtigen Könige, Republiquen.... Jura, Ansprüche etc. beschaffen sey. Lpz. 1716. 2 vols. fol. vellum. *Fine copy.* 7.50

637 — Selecta scripta illustrata, welche viel wichtige in casuis publicis ergangene Materien in sich halten, die nicht allein des H. Röm. Reichs Ober-haupt sondern auch dessen Glieder, ... die freye Reichs-Ritterschaft betreffen. Lpz. 1723. fol. vellum. *Fine copy.* 15.—

638 — Collectio nova, worinn der Mittelbahren, oder Landsäszigen Ritterschaft in Teutsch land, welche unter dem Kayser, auch Chur-Fürsten und Herren angesessin, und von der unmittelbahren freyen Kayserl. Reichs Ritterschaft in Schwaben, Francken, und am Reinstrom, unterschieden ist. Franckf. 1730. 2 vols. in 1. fol. vellum. Stout vol. of 3000 pp. 25.—

639 — Collectio nova, worinn der mittelbahren, oder landsässigen Ritterschaft in Teutschland sonderbahre Praerogativen u. Gerechtsame, etc. enthalten sind. Franckfurt, 1730. 2 vols. fol. Hfcalf. 30.—

640 **Lycklama à Nyeholt, M.,** Membranarum ll. VII, in quibus ad constitutiones codicis et novellarum.... commentarii. Ed. 2a. Leowardia, J. H. Prigge, 1644. 4to. vellum. 5.—

641 **Mably, de,** Oeuvres complètes. Lyon, 1792. 12 vols. calf. 30.—

642 **Machiavelli, N.,** Tutte le opere, divise in V parti. S. l. 1550. 4to. calf. (back damaged). 70.—

First issue of the original edition. There exist many reprints with the same date.

643 — **(Gentillet, I.),** De regno adversus Nic. Machiavellum. L. B., H. de Vogel, 1647. 12mo. Hfvellum. 7.50

644 **Madvig, J. N.,** Die Verfassung und Verwaltung des römischen Staates. Lpz. 1881, 82. 2 vols. in 1. Hfcalf. (Binding broken). 4.—

645 **Maine, H. S.,** Ancient law: its connection with the early history of society, and its relation to modern ideas. London, 1876. cloth. 4.50

646 — Lectures on the early history of institutions. London, 1880. cloth. 4.50

647 **Maioranus, F.,** Opopraxis iudiciaria criminalis. Neap. 1677. fol. vellum. 5.—

648 **Majansius, G.,** Disputationes juris in quibus multa juris civilis ill. Lugd. Bat. 1752. 2 vols. 4to. vellum. 7.50

649 — Ad XXX jurisconsultorum omnia fragmenta, quae exstant in juris civilis corpore, comment. Geneve, 1764. 2 vols. in 1. W. portrait. 4to. vellum. 5.—

650 **Malingre,** Traicté de la loy salique, armes, blasons et devises des François. Paris, 1614. Hfcalf. 7.50

651 **Malte, H. F. de,** Les nobles dans les tribunaux. Traité de droit enrichi de plusieurs curiositez utiles de l'histoire et du blazon. Liege, 1680. fol. calf. 18.—

Contains: Des armoiries, et de leur origine. — Des seaux et cachets. — Du mariage. — Des traitez de mariage. — Des enfans. — etc. .

652 **Mangilius, J. A.,** De evictionibus. Ven. 1654. fol. vellum. (back damaged). 3.75

653 — — The same. Lugd. 1668. fol. vellum. 5.—

654 — De subhastationibus et licitationibus, cum decis. Sacrae rotae Rom. Bracciani, 1636. fol. Hfcalf. (Binding damaged). 3.—

655 — — The same. Ven. 1667. fol. vellum. 4.—

656 **Manns, F.,** Von der mora. Ein Fragment. Frankf. 1878. 1.—

657 **Mantica, F.,** De conjecturis ultimarum voluntatum. Ed. recog. et duct. Geneva, 1645. fol. vellum. 7.50

658 **Manzius, G.,** De testamento valido vel invalido. Ed. 2a. Francof. 1681. fol. calf. 3.50

659 — — The same. Ed. 4a. Bon. 1843. fol. Hfcalf. 2.50

660 **Maranus, G.,** Opera omnia s. paratitla digest. et varii tractatus jur. civil. Rec. C. H. Trotz. Ultraj., J. Broedelet, 1741. W. portrait. folio. vellum. 8.—

661 **Marchesanus, J. B.,** Commissionum ac rescriptorum utriusque signaturae S. D. N. Papae praxis. Romae, 1615. 3 vols. in 2. fol. vellum. (Binding of 1 vol. damaged). 7.50

662 **Marecht, G.,** Studien über die Entwickelung der Verwaltungslehre in Deutschland von der 2en Halfte des 17. b. z. Ende des 18. Jahrh. München, 1885. 6.—

663 **Marckart, J. W.,** Exercit. acad. cum publicitum privati juris. Harderv., W. Brinkink, 1751. 4to. vellum. 4.50

Contains: De suffragio et archiofficis electorali reginae Bohemiae, etc.

664 **Marcou, E.,** L'autorisation maritale au 13e siècle comparée à celle du code civil. Paris, 1899. 5.—

665 **Marees, S. L. E. de,** Untersuchung der Verbindlichkeit der göttlichen Gesetze von der Todesstrafe des Mörders und von Vermeidung blutschänderischer Heyrathen. Dessau, 1771. Hfcalf. 12.—

666 **Marescottus, H.,** Variae resolutiones. Romae, 1614. 2 vols. in 1. vellum. 6.—

667 **Margarita** variarum conclusionum cum ampliat. J. Feliv' et Cerezo. Neap. 1641. fol. vellum. 7.50

668 **Marquardt, J.,** Tractatus polit.-juridicus de jure mercatorum et commerciorum singulari. Francof., Th. M. Götzius, 1662. 2 vols. in 1. W. the rare front. fol. vellum. 175.—

Asher, nr. 42. Extremely important work for the history of commercial law, containing contributions rel. to the commerce of the East and West Indies and the different commercial companies. Nearly all the original documents published in this work are now lost.

Contains a.o.: Argonautica Gustaviana c. extractu W. Wsselincx (publ. 1633). (168 pp.). — Privilegia der West-Indischen Compagnie nacher Musschen Statten ertheilet. — Priviligium Suecicum Gustav I regis vor den Lübeckern und Dantzigern erworben. — Ordnung des in Ruszland residir. Kaufmanns. — Vertrag der Stadt Antwerpen, mit denen da selbst residir. Kaufherren. — etc.

The work has become very scarce.

669 **Marta,** De iurisdictione per et inter iudicem. Avenione, 1669. 2 vols. in 1. fol. vellum. 5.—

670 **Martinez Marina, F.,** Teoria de las Cortes o grandes juntas nacionales de los reinos de Leon y Castilla. Monumentos de su constitucion politica y de la soberania del pueblo. C. observac. s. la lei fundamental.... Española, ... de 1812. Madrid, 1813. 3 vols. 4to. calf. 18.—

See: Prescott, Ferdinand and Isabella, passim. Vol. III contains documents of the years 1340–1611.

671 **Mascardus, J.,** De probationibus. Francof. 1619. 3 vols. fol. oaken boards covered with stamped calf. 12.50

672 **Massa, A.,** De exercitatione iurisperitorum ll. III. Ven., Stella Iordanus Ziletus, 1565. sm. 8vo. calf. (back broken). 4.50

673 **Masuer,** La practique. Mise en françois par A. Fontanon. Nouv. éd. augm. par P. Guenoys. Paris, 1606. 4to. calf. 12.—

674 **Maugis, E.,** Histoire du parlement de Paris de l'avènement des rois Valois à la mort d'Henri IV. Paris, 1913–16. 3 vols. 10.—
675 **Mauléon, Loyseau de,** Plaidoyers et mémoires. Londres, 1780. 3 vols. calf. 4.50
676 **Maurer, G. L. von,** Das Stadt- und das Landrechtsbuch Ruprechts von Freysing. Beitrag zur Geschichte des Schwabenspiegels. Stuttg. 1839. boards. 9.—
677 — — Einleitung zur Geschichte der Mark-, Hof-, Dorf- und Stadt-Verfassung und der öffentlichen Gewalt. München, 1854. boards. 7.50
678 — Geschichte der Markenverfassung in Deutschland. Erlangen, 1856. Hfcalf. 7.50
679 — — Geschichte der Fronhöfe, der Bauernhöfe und der Hofverfassung in Deutschland. Erlangen, 1862–63. 4 vols. Hfcalf. 45.—
680 — Geschichte der Städteverfassung in Deutschland. Erlangen, 1869–71. 4 vols. boards. 35.—
681 **Maximes** du droit public françois. (Rédigées par l'abbé Cl. Mey). S. l. 1772. 2 vols. sm. 8vo. calf. gilt back. 10.—
682 **Mayer, E.,** Italienische Verfassungsgeschichte von der Gothenzeit bis zur Zunftherrschaft. Lpz. 1909. 2 vols. 12.—
683 **Mean, C. de,** Observatt. et res judicatae ad jus civile Leodiensium, Roman., aliarumque gentium. Ed. 3a. Leodii, 1740–41. 8 vols. in 4. W. front. and portr. fol. calf. 20.—
684 **Medices, C. M.,** Decisiones rotae et fori ordinarii Senensis cum additionibus. Ed. 2a. Flor. 1665. 2 vols. in 1. fol. vellum. 5.—
685 **Meiern, J. G. von,** Gedancken von der Rechtmäszigkeit des sechsten Zinsz-Thalers in Deutschland .Schwobach, 1733. 4to. Hfvellum. 3.50
686 **Meister, A.,** Deutsche Verfassungsgeschichte von den Anfängen bis ins 15. Jahrh. 3e Aufl. Berlin, 1922. bound. 1.25
687 **Menagius, A.,** Juris civilis amoenitates ad Lud. Nublaeum.... in quibus plurimae jurisconsultorum leges et veterum autorum loci notantur et emendantur. Ed. 5a. Ultraj., J. Wagens, 1725. W. portrait. sm. 8vo. vellum. 4.50
688 **Menochius, J.,** De arbitrariis judicum quaestionibus et causis. Col. Agrip. 1615. fol. calf. (Binding repaired). 15.—
689 — Commentaria. Colon. Agrip. 1628. fol. calf. 10.—
690 — De adipiscenda et retinenda possessione. Ed. 3a. Ven., Haeredes J. B. Somaschi, 1592. fol. vellum. 3.50
691 — — The same. — **Id.,** In omnes recup. possess. constitut. comment. Ven., J. B. Somaschus, 1576. — 2 vols. in 1. fol. vellum. 5.—
692 — — The same. Item, Responsa causae finariensis. Col. Allobr. 1629. fol. vellum. 5.—
693 — — The same. Geneva, 1687. fol. vellum. 4.—
694 **Merenda, A.,** Controversiarum jurid. ll. XXIV. Brux. 1745–46. 4 vols. in 5. W. 2 portraits. fol. calf. 20.—
695 **Mérilhou, F.,** Les parlements de France, leur caractère politique depuis Philippe le Bel jusqu'en 1789. Paris, 1863. Hfcalf. 6.—
696 **Merlinus, M.,** De legitima; cum decis. S. rotae Romanae. Ven. 1651. fol. vellum. (back damaged). 3.50
697 — De pignoribus et hypothecis, c. decis. s. rotae Rom. Genevae, 1651. fol. vellum. 3.50
698 — — The same. Genevae, 1661. fol. vellum. (back damaged). 3.50
699 — — The same. Ven. 1672. fol. bound. 3.—
700 — — The same. Ed. 3a. Col. Allobr. 1742. fol. vellum. 4.—
701 **Meunier, P.,** Droit romain. De la représentation en matière commerciale maritime. Droit français. Du pilotage. Paris, 1894. 4.50
702 **Mevius, D.,** Comment. in ius Lubecense. Francof. 1664. W. front. folio. vellum. 15.—
Pp. 217 etc.: Der Erbaren Hansee-Städte Schiffs-Ordnung und Seerecht.
703 — Rechtl. Bedencken in Contributions- und Exemtions-Sachen.... ob die von der Ritterschaft wegen ihrer Adel-Standes einig Privilegium vor andern Land-Ständen, sonderlich aber denen von Städten in Contributionibus praetendiren. Zelle, 1720. 4to. boards. 6.—
704 **Meyers, E. M.,** Le droit ligurien de succession en Europe occidentale. I: Les pays alpins. Haarlem, 1928. cloth. 20.—
Rechtshistor. Institut, Leiden. Série II, 2.
705 — Het Ligurische erfrecht in de Nederlanden. Haarlem, 1929–36. Vol. 1–3. 3 vols. W. 2 maps. cloth. 46.25
I. Het West-Brabantsche erfrecht. 17.50. — II. Het West-Vlaamsche erfrecht. 12.75. — III. Het Oost-Vlaamsche erfrecht. 16.—.
Rechtshistor. Instituut, Leiden. Série II, vol. III, V, VII.

706 **Meyers, E. M.**, et **A. S. de Blécourt,** Le droit coutumier de Cambrai. Haarlem, 1932. cloth. 12.75
Rechtshistorisch Instituut, Leiden. Série II, 4.

707 — et **J. J. Salverda de Grave,** Des lois et coutumes de Saint-Amand. Haarlem, 1934. cloth. 12.75
Rechtshistorisch Instituut, Leiden. Serie II, 6.

708 — **Responsa** doctorum tholosanorum ed. E. M. Meijers. Haarlem, 1938. cloth. 15.—
Rechtshist. Instituut, Leiden. Serie II, 8.

709 **Michalorius, B.,** De fratribus add. decis. s. rotae Rom. — **Id.,** De positionibus. — Ven. 1675, 81. 2 vols. in 1. fol. vellum. 4.50

710 — — The same. Ven. 1709. 2 vols. in 1. fol. (Binding damaged). 4.50

711 **Michelsen, A. L. J.,** Die Hausmarke. Jena, 1853. W. 3 pl. 1.50

712 **Miglioruccus, L. B.,** Institut. juris canonici c. explicat. Pisis, 1712–23. 4 vols. 4to. vellum. 10.—

713 **Milovanowitch, M.,** Droit romain: Des sui heredes d'après le droit civil primitif. — Droit français: Des traités de garantie en droit international. Paris, 1888. 7.50

714 **Mitteis, H.,** Rechtsfolgen des Leistungsverzug beim Kaufvertrag nach niederländischen Quellen des Mittelalters. Heidelb. 1913. 1.25
Deutschrechtl. Beiträge. Bd. VIII, 2.

715 — Römisches Privatrecht bis auf die Zeit Diokletians. I: Grundbegriffe und Lehre von den juristischen Personen. Lpz. 1908. (System. Handb. d. dtschen Rechtsw. I, 6). 20.—
All published. Scarce.

716 **Molieres-Fonmaur, B. L.,** Traité des droits de lods et ventes, selon le droit commun du royaume. Lyon, 1783. 2 vols. in 1.4to. calf. 6.—

717 **Moneta, J. P.,** De conservatoribus iudicibus. Lugd. 1619. 4to. boards. 3.75

718 **Montanus, H.,** Controversiae forenses ad consuetudines Neapolitanas. Neap. 1643. fol. Hfvelum. 6.50

719 **Montanus, P., J. Guttierez** et **B. Cavalcanus,** De tutore, curatore, et usufructu mulieri relicto. Aug. Taurin. 1611. fol. vellum. 5.—

720 — — The same. Geneva, 1675. folio. vellum. 7.50

721 **Monte Brixianus, H. de,** De finibus regendis civitatum, castrorum.... tam urban. quam rustic. Ven. 1556. limp vellum. 4.50
Several words underlined.

722 **(Montesquieu),** De l'esprit des loix, ou du rapport que les loix doivent avoir avec la constitution de chaque gouvernement, les moeurs, le climat, la religion, le commerce, etc. Leyde, 1749. 2 vols. in 1. 4to. calf, gilt back, gilt edges. *Fine copy.* 35.—

723 **Monzambano, Sev. de** (= S. Pufendorf), De statu imperii Germanici. Acc. scholia a Chr. Thomasio. Halae Magd. 1703.
The first important work of Pufendorf containing a severe criticism on the German constitution.

W. von Schroeder, Fürstliche Schatz- und Rent-Kammer, nebst unterricht vom Goldmachen. Lpz. 1704.
Early edition of this famous work.

Chr. Thomas, Von der Kunst vernünfftig zu lieben, oder Einleitung zur Sitten-Lehre. 3. (Aufl.). Halle (ab. 1703).

Chr. Thomas, Von der Artzeney wider die unvernünfftige Liebe.... oder Ausübung der Sittenlehre. 3. verb. Aufl. Halle, 1704.

Tog. 4 works in 1 stout vol. vellum. 75.—

724 **Morhof, D. G.,** Delitiae oratoriae intimioris. Lubecae, 1701. 2.50

725 **Mortreuil, J. A. B.,** Histoire du droit byzantin ou du droit romain dans l'empire d'Orient depuis le mort de Justinien jusqu'à la prise de Constantinople en 1453. Paris, 1843–46. 3 vols. Hfcalf. 75.—
Very important work, of the utmost rarity.

726 **Mosconius, L.,** Dilucidationes totius iuris civilis. Bon. 1615. fol. vellum. 5.—

727 **Moser, F. C. von,** Regenten, Regierung und Ministers. Frankf. a. M. 1784. sm. 8vo. calf. 6.—
Original edition.

728 **(—)** Ueber den Diensthandel deutscher Fürsten. Frankfurt, 1786. sm. 8vo. 6.—

729 **Moser, J. J.,** Teutsches Staats-Recht. Nürnberg, 1737–54. 50 vols. in 25. W. „Zusätze", 2 vols. in 1 and 1 vol. of tables. Tog. 53 vols. in 27. 4to. vellum. (2 bindings slightly damaged). 600.—

Complete copy of this fundamental work. See for the great importance of this work, which very rarely is offered, especially in complete condition: Allgem. Deutsche Biographie. Bd. XXII, p. 376.

730 — — Von der Landeshoheit im Weltlichen; und zwar in Regierungs-Sachen; in Justiz Sachen, Militar-Sachen, in Sachen welche Erde, Wasser betreffen, u.s.w. Lpz. 1772. 4to. calf. 6.—

731 — Von der Landeshoheit derer Teutschen Reichsstände überhaupt nach denen Reichs gesezen. Mit Nachricht von allen öffentl. Staatsgeschäfften. Lpz. 1773. 4to. calf. 6.—

732 **Müller, Ph. F.,** De via publica. Von freyer Land- und Heerstrassen. Itemq; De juribus eidem annexis. Helmestadii, 1677. 4to. 2.50

733 **Muyart de Vouglans, P. F.,** Institutes au droit criminel, ou principes généraux sur ces matières. Av. traité particulier des crimes. Paris, 1757. 4to. calf. 8.50

734 — Les loix criminelles de France, dans leur ordre naturel. Paris, 1780. fol. calf. 15.—

„Ouvrage écrit d'après les Vieux principes d'inquisition et de tortures. Il combattit contre le système de Montesquieu, touchant la modération des peines." Dupin.

735 **Naber, J. C.,** De vormende kracht v. h. Rom. recht. Utrecht, 1885. 1.—

736 **Naevius, S.,** Systema selectorum ius Justin. et feudale concern. Francof. 1608. 2 vols. in 1. fol. Hfvellum. 5.—

737 **Nerus Badia, J. B.,** Decisiones et responsa iuris, quibus acc. decis. Pompeii Neri. Flor. 1769, 76. 2 vols. fol. Hfvellum. 7.50

738 **Nesmond, A. de,** Remontrances, et ouvertures du palais, et arrests prononcez en robes rouges. 3e éd. Lyon, 1656. 4to. calf. 20.—

739 **Nicolovius, M. B.,** Disputatio juridica de venatione tempore foeturae ferarum prohibita. Von verbothener Jagd zur Setz- und Brut- oder Heg- und Schon-Zeit. Königsberg, 1743. 4to. calf. 6.—

740 **Nider, J.,** Tractatus de contractibus mercatorum. (Esslingen, C. Fijner, ab. 1474–75). 16 ll. W. 2 large initials, painted in red, on first page. fol. Full brown mor. *Fine copy.* 550.—

Hain, nr. 11823. B. M. Cat. IB 8960. Important work on mercantile law. Very rare.

741 — Praeceptorium divinae legis. (Reutlingen, M. Greyff, ab. 1479). oaken boards, covered with leather. 200.—

Hain, nr. 11781. Proctor, nr. 2684. B. M. Cat. IB. 10623.

Fine copy with very wide margins, several of which uncut, in its original binding. (Clasps gone). Leaf 1, 24 and 25 of the index in contemporary ms. Without the first blank leaf.

742 **Niger, A.,** De exceptionibus remorantibus. Romae, 1647. fol. vellum. (Binding damaged). 3.75

743 **Noodt,** Du pouvoir des Souverains, et de la liberté de conscience. Trad. du latin p. J. Barbeyrac. 2e éd. Augm. de plus. notes, ... du discours de J. F. Gronovius sur la loi Roiale; et d'un discours du traducteur sur la nature du sort. Amst., P. Humbert, 1714. W. front. sm. 8vo. calf. 15.—

744 **Novarius, J. M.,** De insolutum bonorum datione. Acc. tract. II J. C. Glusiani. Antv. 1673. fol. vellum. 5.—

745 **Oecumenica** cathedrae apostolicae authoritas ex occas. IV. cleri Gallicani propositionum anno 1682 in Paris. ecclesiast. conventu editarum. No pl. 1689. fol. vellum. 4.50

746 **Oldendorp, J.,** Actionum forensium progymnasmata. Francof. 1608. vellum. 3.—

747 **Olea, A. de,** De cessione iurium et actionum. Roma, 1658. fol. vellum. (back damaged). 5.—

748 **Olim, (Les),** ou registres des arrêts rendus par la cour du roi sous les règnes de St. Louis, de Philippe le Hardi, de Philippe le Bel, de Louis le Hutin et de Philippe le Long. Publ. p. Beugnot. Paris, 1839–48. 3 vols. in 4. 4to. 40.—

Very sought after.

Collection de documents inédits sur l'histoire de France.

749 **d'Olivier, J.,** De la réforme des loix civile. Paris, 1786. 2 vols. calf. 8.50

750 **Onuphrius,** (card. Tuschus), Practicae conclusiones iuris. Romae, 1605–08. 8 vols. W. pl. fol. vellum. (Binding damaged). 25.—

751 **Ordonnance** de la marine 1681. Comment. et conferée sur les anciennes ordonn., le droit romain et les nouveaux réglements. Paris, 1714. 4to. calf. 7.50

752 **Ordonnances des roys de France** de la troisième race. Recueillies par ordre chronolog. Paris, 1723–1849. 21 vol. Av. tables des tom. I–IX et table chronolog. par Pardessus. Tog. 23 vols. fol. calf, gilt back. (2 vols. sewn). 1525.—
Complete set, of the greatest rarity. Bound in 2 bindings, not quite uniform, but in perfect state.

753 **Origine, De l',** du droit d'amortissement par Me Eusèbe de L.**** Paris, 1692. sm. 8vo. calf. 2.50

754 **Ortega, I. J. de,** Questiones del derecho publico en interpretacion de los tratados de paces. Insertanse al fin las cedulas del almirantazgo, y la instruccion dada à los ministros de marina. Madrid, 1747. 4to. limp vellum. 20.—

755 **Ortelius, A.,** Pagage, Das vnrechtmessige.... Rauben vnd Plündern Allen denen Lande Stadt- Dorff- vnd Strassen Raubern, welche.... Vieh nehmen, Kirchen vnd Pfarrhäuser, Städte, Schlösser und Dörffer ausplündern, Pagage- und Mercatender Wägen mit solchen Raubguthe beladen.... zu feilen Kauff bringen. Ingleichen den Kippern vnd Wippern, etc. Dreszden, 1640. W. curious front., represent. a procession of brigands with their plunder, engraved by S. W(eisshuhn?). 4to. boards. 36.—

756 **Osenbrüggen, E.,** Deutsche Rechtsalterthümer aus der Schweiz. Zürich, 1858–59. 3 parts in 1. boards. *Reprint.* 3.—

757 **Otto, E.,** De vita S. Rufi, ejusd. P. Alfenus Varus ab injuriis veterum et recentiorum liberatus. Ultr. 1737. vellum. 1.50

758 **Pacificus, S.,** De Salviano interdicto. Romae, 1617, 18. 2 vols. in 1. fol. vellum. (Binding damaged). 5.—

759 — — The same. Ven. 1656. fol. vellum. 5.—

760 **Pacionus, P.,** Allegationes civiles et canonicae. Col. Allobr. 1700. fol. calf. (Binding damaged). 4.—

761 **Padelletti, G.,** Lehrbuch der römischen Rechtsgeschichte. Deutsche Ausg. von F. von Holtzendorff. Berlin, 1879. Hfcalf. 2.—

762 **Palaeotus, G.,** De nothis spuriisque filiis. Ven., J. Leoncinus, 1572. sm. 8vo. calf. 5.—

763 **Palma, H.,** Consilia. Bon. 1641. fol. vellum. 4.50

764 **Papon, J.,** [Oeuvres]. 5e éd. Lyon, 1617–20. 3 vols. fol. calf. 20.—
I. Instrument du premier notaire. — II. Trias judicial du second notaire. — III. Secrets du troisième et dernier notaire.

765 — Corpus juris Francici, seu collectio arrestorum. Col. Allobr. 1624. — **Afflictis, M. de,** Decisonum sacri regii Neapolitarii consilii. Francof. 1616. — In 1 vol. fol. vellum. 7.50
The end of the „Additiones" is missing.

766 **Pardessus, J. M.,** Collection de lois maritimes antérieures au 18e siècle. Paris, 1828–45. 6 vols. 4to. Hfcalf. 500.—
Very scarce.

767 — Us et coutumes de la mer ou collection des usages maritimes des peuples de l'antiquité et du moyen-âge. Paris, 1847. 2 vols. 4to. Hfcalf. 75.—
Reprint of the chap. I–XIV (= vol. I–II) of the great work „Coll. des lois maritimes, etc.", together with the additions concerning the chapters at the end of vol. VI.

768 — Loi salique ou recueil conten. les anciennes rédactions de cette loi et le texte connu sous le nom de lex emendata. Av. notes et diss. Paris, 1843. 4to. Hfcalf. 30.—
Copy with annotations and marginal corrections.

769 **Parexa, G. de,** Praxis edendi s. de universa instrumentorum editione. Lugd. 1668. 2 vols. in 1. fol. vellum. 4.—

770 **Paris, J.,** La responsabilité de la custodia en droit romain. Paris, 1926. 3.—

771 **Pasquier, E.,** Les recherches de la France. Ed. augm. de 3 livres. Paris, 1643. fol. calf. 10.—

772 — — The same. Paris, 1665. W. portrait. fol. calf. (rebacked). 28.—
Esteemed edition.

773 **Passarellus, A.,** De donationibus. Ferrar. 1673. fol. vellum. 6.—

774 **Passerinus, P. F.,** De occidente unum pro alio. Parmae, 1693. fol. vellum. 4.—

775 **Pastoret, de,** Histoire de la législation. Paris, 1817–37. 11 vols. Hfcalf. (8–11 sewn). 50.—

776 **Patru,** Plaidoyers et oeuvres diverses. Nouv. éd. augm. Paris, 1681. calf. 4.50
This learned work contains the legislation of the ancient civilisations: Assyria, Egypt, Palestine, Athens, etc.

777 — Oeuvres. Ses playdoyers, harangues, etc. Amst., G. Gallet, 1692. 2 vols. in 1. W. front. sm. 8 vo. Hfcalf. 6.—

778 **Paulutius, M. A.,** Dissert. legales recoll. per Th. Torellus. Lucae, 1707, 11. 2 vols. fol. vellum. (Binding damaged). 6.—

779 **Pecchius, F. M.,** De servitutibus in genere. — **Id.,** De servitutibus urbanis. — Flor. 1839. 2 vols. in 1. fol. Hfvellum. 2.50

780 — De aquaeductu. Flor. 1840. 2 vols. in 1. fol. Hfvellum. 3.—

781 **Peckius, P.,** Opera omnia. Antv. 1647. fol. vellum. 20.—
Pp. 815–896: Ad rem nauticam.

782 **Pecquet,** Loix forestières de France, commentaire historique et raisonné sur l'ordonance de 1669, les règlemens antérieures, et ceux qui l'ont suivie; auquel on a joint une bibliothèque des auteurs qui ont écrit sur les matières d'eaux et forêts, et une notice des coutumes. Paris, 1753. 2 vols. 4to. calf. 24.—

783 **Peregrinus, M. A.,** Tractatus varii. Ven. 1611. fol. Hfvellum. 5.—

784 **Perez, A.,** Institut. imperiales erotematibus distinctae. Ed. nov. Noviom., A. ab Hoogenhuysen, 1662. W. front. 12mo. calf, with coats of arms. 3.50

785 **Pernice, A.,** Labeo. Das römische Privatrecht im ersten Jahrh. der Kaiserzeit. Halle, 1873–78. Vol. I. — Idem. Vol. II. Erste Abt. et II. Abt. II, 1. (2te neu bearbeitete Aufl.). 1895–1900. — **Idem.** Vol. III. Erste Abt. 1892. Tog. 3 vols. boards. 60.—
Complete set, best edition.

786 **Pernice, L.,** Geschichte, Alterthümer und Institut. des röm. Rechts im Grundrisse. 2e Aufl. Halle, 1824. bound. 1.25

787 **Phedericus, S. de,** De interpretatione juris. Francof., Chr. Aegenolph, 1535.
— **Die Lehenrecht** verdeutscht; auch im neyn neuwe und richtige ordnung der Tittel gefatzt unnd zusamen bracht. Wormbs, S. Wagner, 1536.
— **Rotweilisch Hoffgericht.** Ordenung unnd sundere Gesatz des H. Röm. Reichs Hoffgericht zu Rotweil. Franckfurt, Chr. Egenolff, 1535. W. woodcut on titlepage and portrait of King Conrad.
— **Gerichts ordenung** der Graveschafft Nassaw. Wormbs, S. Wagner, 1535. W. woodcut on titlepage. *Scarce.*
— **Meintzisch hoffgerichts Ordnung** zu allen andern gerichten dienlich. Meintz, J. Schöffer, 1521. W. title in woodcutborder.
— **Gerichts ordnung, Keyser Karls V. unnd des H. Röm. Reichs peinlich,** auff den Reichsztagen zu Augspurgk und Regenspurgk 1532 gehalten, auffgericht und beschlossen. Meyntz, J. Schöffer, 1534. W. woodcut on titlepage and 1 woodcut in the text.
In 1 vol. fol. stamped pigskin. 200.—
Collection of 6 important works.

788 **Pfeffel,** Nouvel abrégé chronolog. de l'histoire et du droit public d'Allemagne. Paris, 1776. 2 vols. 4to. Hfcalf. 6.—

789 **Pfeiffer, B. W.,** Das deutsche Meierrecht nach seiner rechtlichen Begründung und dermaligen Gestaltung. Kassel, 1848. boards. 6.—

790 **Phillimore, J. C.,** Private law among the Romans from the Pandects. London, 1863. cloth. 2.50

791 **Pichler S. J., V.,** Jus canonicum practice explicatum. Ingolst. 1746. fol. calf. 5.—

792 **Pinault, M.,** Histoire du Parlement de Tournay. Valenciennes, 1701. W. portr. 4to. calf. 4.50

793 **Pigeau,** La procedure civile du Châtelet de Paris et de toutes les jurisdictions ordonaires du royaume. Paris, 1779. 2 vols. 4to. calf. 7.50

794 **Pinault, M.,** Recueil d'arrets notables du Parlement de Tournay. Valenciennes, 1702–05. 4 vols. in 2. 4to. calf. 12.—

795 — Recueil d'arrets notables du Parlement de Tournay (*vol. 3 and 4 are entitled*:) Suite des arrests notables du Parlement de Flandres). Valenciennes, Douay, 1702–15. 4 vols. 4to. calf. 15.—

796 **Pinu, L. de,** Consilia s. responsa. Ven., F. Zilettus, 1579. fol. vellum. 6.50

797 **Pitonius, F. M.,** Disceptiones ecclesiasticae (LIII). Romae, 1704. 2 vols. fol. vellum. 5.—

798 — — The same. (Disc. CLX). Ven. 1733. 4 vols. in 3. fol. Hfvellum. 7.50

799 — — The same. Ven. 1742–46. 4 vols. in 2. fol. vellum. 7.50

800 **Planck, J. W.,** Das Deutsche Gerichtsverfahren im Mittelalter. Brschw. 1878, 1879. 2 vols. bound. 12.—

801 **Planitz, H.,** Die Vermögungsvollstreckung im deutschen mittelalterlichen Recht. I. Die Pfändung. Lpz. 1912. bound. 10.—
Out of print. All published.

802 **Pocquet, C.,** Traité des fiefs. 5e éd. Paris, 1771. 4to. calf. 10.—
The best edition.

803 **Pontius, B.,** De sacramento matrimonii. Ven. 1756. fol. Hfvellum. 4.—

804 **Postius, L.,** Mandati de manutenendo. Ed. 2a. Col. Allobr. 1646. 2 vols. in 1. fol. vellum. 5.—
805 — — The same. Acc. tract. de Boccatiis a Cingulo de interdicto uti possidetis, etc. Lugd. 1717. fol. vellum. 6.—
806 **Potestate, De,** summi magistratus. Authore A. A. F. de C. H. L. S. T. L. Antverp, 1632. sm. 8vo. vellum. 3.50
807 **Prematica** en que se manda guardar la en que se dio la forma en la labor de las sedas, y se declara el peso que ha de tener cada bara. Madrid, Tomas de Junta, 1595. sm. fol. 18.—
808 **Preudhomme,** Traité des droits aux seigneurs sur les biens possédés en roture. Paris, 1781. 4to. calf. 10.—
809 **Privilegien** statuyten ende reglementen van Hasselt. Hasselt, (1716). 4to. calf, with the coals of arms of Hasselt. 7.50
810 **Procès-verbal** des conférences tenues pour l'examen des articles de l'ordonnance civile. de 1667 et de l'ordonnance criminelle de 1670. Nouv. ed. augm. Paris, 1776. 4to. calf. 6.—
811 **Project** des codicis Fridericiani Marchici, oder, eine nach S. Mäj. von Preussen selbst vorgeschriebenen Plan entworffene Cammer- Gerichts-Ordnung, nach welcher alle Processe in einem Jahr durch drey Instantzen zum Ende gebracht werden sollen. Berlin, 1749. 4to. vellum. 7.50
812 **Puntschart, P.,** Schuldvertrag und Treugelöbnis des Sächsischen Rechts im Mittelalter. Lpz. 1896. bound. 12.—
Out of print.
813 **Pütter, (J. S.),** Historische Entwickelung der heutigen Staatsverfassung des Teutschen Reichs. Gött. 1788. 3 vols. boards. 12.—
814 — Litteratur des Teutschen Staatsrechts. Gött. 1776–83. 3 vols. Hfcalf. 12.—
815 **Ramos, J. F.,** Tribonianus s. errores Triboniani de poena parricidii. L. B., J. vander Aa, 1728. W. 3 pl. 4to. vellum. 5.—
816 **Ramos del Manzano, F.,** Ad leges Juliam et Papiam, comment. etc. Matr. 1678. W. portrait. fol. Hfcalf. 6.—
817 **Rauch, K.,** Spurfolge und Anefang in ihren Wechselbeziehungen. Beitrag z. Geschichte der deutschen Fahrnisprozesses. Weimar, 1908. 1.50
818 **(Rausinus, G.),** Ad sacratiss. Caesaream Maiestatem inclytae civitatis Leodiensis delegatio. Leod. 1629. 4to. 2.50
819 **Raynaldus, J. D.,** Vota. Roma, 1714. fol. vellum. 4.50
820 — Observat. criminales, civiles, etc. — **Id.,** Vota. Ven. 1735. 4 vols. in 2. fol. vellum. 6.—
821 **Raynouard,** Histoire du droit municipal en France, sous la domination romaine et sous les trois dynasties. Paris, 1829. 2 vols. Hfcalf. 4.50
822 **Recht, Das alte Bamberger,** als Quelle der Carolina. Nach bisher ungedruckten Urkunden und Hss. hrsg. von H. Zoepfl. Heidelberg, 1839. boards. 8.50
823 **Recht, Das alte Lübische.** Hrsg. von J. F. Hach. Lübeck, 1839. boards. 12.50
824 **Rechten,** en costumen van Antwerpen. Antw., Chr. Plantijn, 1582. W. map. fol. vellum cover. 30.—
Bound up with: Ordonnantie ende verhael vanden stijl, ende maniere van procederen, voor amptman, borghemeester, ende schepenen van Antwerpen. Antw., Chr. Plantijn, 1582.
„Livre d'une belle ordonnance typographique: grand caractère gothique amples marges. L'ouvrage ne put pas livré au commerce et le magistrat ne fit distribuer des exemplaires qu'aux fonctionnaires et aux notables de la ville."
825 **Rechten,** ende costumen v. Antwerpen. Amst., H. Barentssz., 1607. — **Ordonnantie** v. d. stijl v. procedeeren. No pl. 1607. — **By-voechsel** v. d. costumen v. Antwerpen. Ceulen, 1607. — **Blyde incomste** den hertochdomme v. Brabant verleent, 1549. Ceulen, 1607. — In 1 vol. 4to. vellum. 12.—
826 **Rechten** ende costuymen der hooft-bancke van Santhoven. Antw. 1727. 4to. vellum. 12.—
827 **Rechtsbuch, Das,** n. Distinctionen nebst e. Eisenachischen Rechtsbuch. Hrsg. von Fr. Ortloff. Jena, 1836. bound. 3.—
828 **Rechtskritik** des Amicistenorders n. der histor. Anleit. im Graf Guido von Taufkirchen und allgemeingült. Rechtsgrundsätzen für alle geheime Ordens-Gesellschaften. Chemn. 1800. sm. 8vo. 2.—
829 **Rechtssprichwörter, Deutsche,** unter Mitwirkung von J. C. Bluntschli und K. Maurer gesammelt und erklärt von E. Graf und M. Diethen. 2e Ausg. Nördl. 1869. bound. 24.—
Very scarce.

830 **Rechtsurkunden, Assyrische,** in Umschrift und Uebersetzung von J. Kohler und A. Ungnad. Lpz. 1913. cloth. 17.50

831 **Recopilacion, Novisima,** de las leyes de España. En que se reforma la recopilacion publ. por Felipe II en 1567, y se incorporan las pragmaticas, cedules, decretos, etc. no recopiladas, y expedidas hasta el de 1804. Madrid, 1805–07. 6 vols. in 4. fol. calf. 30.—

832 **Recueil** des actes des Comtes de Pontieu (1026–1279). Publ. p. C. Brunel. Paris, 1930. W. map and 4 pl. royal 4to. (778 pp.). 12.50

Forms a part of: Collection de documents inédits sur l'histoire de France.

833 **Recueil** des anciens ordonnances et coutumes de la Belgique. Publ. par la Commission Royale pour la publication des anciennes lois et otdonnances de la Belgique. Brux. 1855–1936. 102 stout vols. fol. and 4to. 575.—

Complete collection of this very important publication.

834 **Recueil** des arrests et reglements sur le faict de la jurisdiction et compétence de la vicomté de Leauë à Roüen. Av. l'arrest conten. l'ordre des decrets des batteaux. Rouen, 1623. sm. 8vo. vellum. (Modern binding). 10.—

835 **Recueil** d'édits et d'ordonnances royaux, sur le fait de la justice e.a. matières les plus importantes. Augm. sur l'éd. de P. Neron et E. Girard. Paris, 1720. 2 vols. fol. calf. 20.—

Contains the ordonnances of the kings Philip VI, John I, Charles V, a.o. till Lewis XIV.

836 **Redenaschus, F.,** Consilia. Ticinum Regium, 1652. W. portrait. fol. vellum. 4.50

837 **Redoanus, G.,** De alienationibus rerum ecclesiarum. Ed. 9a. Placentiae, J. Bazachius, 1589. fol. limp vellum. 5.—

838 **Regnaud, G.,** Droit romain. Du colonat. Droit français. Des abordages maritimes. Paris, 1891. Hfcalf. 7.50

839 **Rehm, H.,** Geschichte der Staatsrechtswissenschaft. Freibg. 1896. cloth. 6.—

840 **Rei agrariae** auctores legesque variae prod. cura W. Goesii c. notis etc. N. Rigallii. Amst. 1674. W. front., pl. and ill. 4to. vellum. 4.—

841 **Rein, A.,** Drei Uerdinger Weisthümer a. d. J. 1454. Crefeld, 1854. 1.—

842 **Rein, W.,** Das römische Privatrecht und der Civilprozess bis in das erste Jahrh. der Kaiserherrschaft. Lpz. 1836. boards. ?.—

843 **Reinkingk, T.,** Tractatus synopticus de retractu consanguinitatis. Acc. responsum juris. Francof. 1670. W. front. 4to.vellum. 6.50

Bound up with: **Sanz a Morquecho ,P.,** Practica quotidiana. De divisione bonorum. Francof. 1607.

844 **Relationes, Vermehrte,** et casus criminales cum rationibus dubitandi et decidendi, d. H. W. v. L. (In German). Zelle, 1721. 4to. 4.—

845 **Renauldon, J.,** Dictionnaire des fiefs et des droits seigneuriaux utiles et honorifiques. Paris, 1765. 4to. calf. 6.—

846 — Traité histor. et pratique des droits seigneuriaux de France. Paris, 1765. 4to. calf. 6.50

847 **Renusson, De,** Oeuvres, conten. le traité de la communauté de biens entre l'homme et la femme, le traité du douaire, etc. Nouv. éd. p. J. A. Serieux. Paris, 1760. Bound in 2 vols. fol. calf. 10.—

848 **Resolutiones** wegen Abstell- und Remedirung derer in Bergwercks-Sachen gekommenen und angemerckten Mängel und Gebrechen, sonderlich die Freybergische Revier betreffend, dato 7. Januar 1709. So wohl die Freybergische neue Schmiede-Taxe worbey zugleich die vormahlige Berg-Decrete von 1624, 1629 and 1659. Dresden (1709). — **Declaration** wegen erhöheter Berg- Brand- Silber-Bezahlung und Ertz-Taxe. Dreszden, 1765. — In 1 vol. sm. fol. Hfcalf. 10.—

849 **Revue Catholique de droit** p. E. Crahay. Louvain, 1898–1914. Year 1–17. 17 vols. 11 of which hfcalf, rest in parts. 75.—

Titlepages and index to vol. 15 and 16 not published.
All published.

850 **Revue d'histoire du droit.** Sous la dir. de A. S. de Blécourt, J. v. Kan, J. v. Kuyk, E. M. Meijers. Av. le concours de R. Altamira y Crevea, E. Cuq, J. Jörgensen, E. Meynial, V. Scialoja, J. H. Wigmore, e.a. Haarlem, 1918–37. Vol. 1–15. 15 vols. cloth. 300.—

Contributions in english, french, italian, etc. Vol. 1 and 2 were entitled: Tijdschrift voor rechtsgeschiedenis.

851 **Revue d'histoire diplomatique,** publiée par la Société d'histoire diplomatique. Paris, 1887–1936. Vol. 1–50. 50 vols. unif. hfcalf. 650.—

852 **Ribéreau, A.,** Théorie de l'„in bonis habere", ou de la propriété prétorienne. Paris, 1867. 1.25

853 **Ricard, J. M.,** Traité des donations entrevifs et testamentaires. Av. la coutume d'Amiens commentée. Paris, 1734. 2 vols. fol. calf. 7.—
854 — — The same. Riom, 1783. 2 vols. fol. calf. (Bindings rubbed). 45.—
At the end: Coutumes du baillage de Senlis et d'Amiens.
The best and most complete edition. Extremely scarce.
855 **Ricciardus, P.,** De obligationibus. Ven., Minima Societas, 1593. fol. Hfvellum. 5.—
856 **Riccius, C. G.,** Zuverlasziger Entwurff von Stadt-Gesetzen, oder Statutis vornehmlich der Land-Städte. Franckf. 1740. 4to. boards. 3.—
857 **Richeus, J.,** Vindiciae praetoris Romani et juris honorarii. Lugd. Bat. 1748. 1.—
858 **Richter, C. P.,** De jure et privilegiis creditorum. Ed. 2a. Jenae, 1656. W. front. 4to. vellum. 2.50
859 **Richthofen, K. von,** Friesische Rechtsquellen. Berlin, 1840. W. 1 pl. 4to. boards. 50.—
Very scarce and much sought after.
860 — Untersuch. über Friesische Rechtsgeschichte. Berlin, 1880–86. Vol. I–III, 1. In 3 vol. W. map. Hfcalf. 25.—
All published.
861 **Richtsteig Landrechts, Der,** nebst Cautela und Premis, hrsg. von C. G. Homeyer. Berlin, 1857. Hfcalf. 9.—
862 **Riedel, A. C.,** Beschreibung d. im Fürstenthum Bayreuth zu Sanct Georgen am See errichteten Zucht u. Arbeit-Hauses. Bayr. 1750. 4to. 2.50
Pp. 147–166 contain Wörterb. d. Rothwelschen Wörter u. Redensarten.
863 **Rigantius, J. B.,** Comment. in regulas. constitutiones et ordinationes Cancellariae Apostolicae. Col. Allobr. 1751. 4 vols. in 2. fol. calf. (Librarystamp on titlepages). 8.50
864 **Rintelen, M.,** Schuldhaft und Einlager im Volkstreckungsverfahren des altniederl. u. sächs. Rechtes. Lpz. 1908. 2.50
865 **Rivier, A.,** Untersuch. üb. die cautio praedibus praediisque. Berlin, 1863. 1.—
866 **Robillard de Beaurepaire, G. de,** Du culte des ancêtres chez les Romains dans ses rapports avec le droit privé en droit romain. — Des avaries communes en droit français. Caen, 1890. 6.—
867 **Roccus, F.,** De officiis eorumque regimine. Neap. 1669. W. portrait. fol. vellum. 4.50
868 **Rocha, B.,** Practicabilium iudiciorum tractatus. Ven., J. B. Somaschus, 1586. 4to. vellum. 4.50
869 **Roeder, K. D. A.,** Grundgedanken und Bedeutung des römischen und germanischen Rechts. Lpz. 1855. Hfcloth. 6.—
870 **Rodier, M. A.,** Questions sur l'ordonnance de Louis XIV du mois d'avril 1667 rel. aux usages des cours de parlement, et princip. de celui de Toulouse. Nouv. éd. augm. Toulouse, 1769. 4to. calf. 3.75
871 **Rodiquez, Am.,** De concursu et privilegiis creditorum in bonus debitoris. Ven. 1664. fol. vellum. 6.—
872 **Rodolfinus, L.,** De origine, dignitate et potestate ducum Italiae. Ed. C. Besold. Argent. 1624. 4to. 2.50
873 **Rodulphinus, A.,** Allegationes. Bon. 1693. fol. vellum. 5.—
874 **Rogge, K. A.,** Das Gerichtswesen der Germanen. Halle, 1820. bound. 2.50
875 — — The same. — **F. W. Unger,** Die altdeutsche Gerichts-Verfassung. Gött. 1842. — In 1 vol. boards. 5.—
876 **Ronchegallus, Gioldus J.,** Tractatus de duobus rei constituendis. Venetiis, Cominus de Tridino Montisferrati, 1558. — **Zoanettus, F.,** Repetitio in L. 2 C. de pact. inter empt. et vendit. Add. tractatio de venatione Germanica. Ingolstad, A. et S. Weissenhorn, 1556. — In 1 vol. folio. vellum cover. 30.—
The 2d work with dedication of Zoanethus to Georg Sigism. Seld. Excellmi viro Dño Georgio Sigismundo Seldio.... Caesarisque Procancellario.... et Amico venerando F. Zoanettus....
877 — — The first work only. Ven. 1559. fol. vellum. 10.—
878 **Roques, P.,** Traité des tribunaux de judicature, ou l'on examine ce que la religion exige des juges, des plaideurs, des avocats et des témoins. Basle, 1740. 4to. calf. 4.50
879 **Rosignolus, G.,** De contractibus controversiae. Mediol. 1678. fol. vellum. 3.75
880 — — The same. Ed. 2a. Mediol. 1719. fol. boards. 4.50
881 — De dote controversiae. Mediol. 1691. 2 vols. fol. vellum. 6.—
882 — Novissima praxis in universas de sponsalibus controversias. Ed. 2a. Mediol. 1711. fol. 4.—
883 **Rosinius, J.,** Antiquitatum Roman, corpus absolutiss. C. not. T. Dempsteri, cui acc. P. Manutii: De legibus et de senatu. Amst., S. Schouten, 1743. W. pl. 4to. calf. 5.—

884 **Roulliard, S.**, Les reliefs forenses. 2e éd. Paris, 1610. 2 vols. in 1. 4to. veau. 12.—
„Ce recueil est réellement curieux par la variété et l'importance des cinquante questions qui y sont traitées." Biogr. Univ. 39.

885 **Rovitus, S.**, Luculenta commentaria in singulas regni Neap. pragmaticas sanctiones. Ed. 6a. Acc. addit. J. Laganarii. Neap. 1649. fol. limp vellum. 4.50

886 **Roye, F. de**, De missis dominicis eorum officio et potestate. Recens. I. W. Neuhaus. Lpz. 1744. vellum. 2.—

887 **Rubens, P.**, De validitate legali controversiae. Romae, 1664. fol. vellum. 3.—

888 **Rudorff, A. F.**, Römische Rechtsgeschichte. Lpz. 1857–59. 2 vols. 4.—

889 **Rudorff, H.**, Zur Rechtsstellung der Gäste im mittelalterlichen städtischen Prozess. Vorzugsweise nach norddeutschen Quellen. Breslau, (1907). 2.25
Untersuchungen z. dtschen Staats- und Rechtsgesch. no.88.

890 **Ruginellus, J. C.**, Practicae quaestiones. Ven. 1610. fol. vellum. 4.50

891 **Rusticis, J. de**, An et quando liberi in conditione positi vocentur. Ven. 1587. W. portrait. fol. vellum. 5.—

892 — — The same. Ed. 2a. Ven., Damianus Zenarus, 1598. fol. Hfvellum. 6.—

893 — In A. P. Papiniani responsum ll. IX. Ad l. cum auus de condit. et demonstrat. comment. Ven. 1613. fol. Hfcalf. 4.—

894 **Rutilius, B.**, Iurisconsultorum vitae, noviss. elimitae, et mendis non paucis, quibus scatebant, repurgatae. Lugd., Germanus Rose, 1538. calf. 5.—
The margin of the last leaves has somewhat suffered from water.

895 — **J. Bertrandus** et **G. Grotius**, Vitae tripartitae iurisconsult. vet. Halae, 1718. 3 vols. in 1. W. portr. 4to. calf. 4.50

896 **Sabadie, H.**, Les sources du droit civil espagnol. Carcassonne, 1926. 3.50
Bibl. de l'Institut de droit comparé de Toulouse. Etudes de droit privé espagnol. I.

897 **Sabinus, G.**, Opus elegantissimum, continens consilia et quasdam orationes ac disputationes electorum principum in eligendo Caesare. Coloniae. H. Mameran, 1560. sm. 8vo. limp vellum. (Titlepage damaged and mounted). 7.50
Deals with the election of Charles V, and the second part is an exterior report of the coronation at Aix-la-Chapelle by H. Maurus.

898 **Sainct Mauris, F. de**, La pratique et stil judiciaire tant en la cour de parlement, qu'es tribunaux de justice au comté de Bourgogne. Rev. et augm. (p. Boivin). Dole, 1626. 4to. calf. (Binding rubbed). 5.—

899 **Saint-Génois, J. de**, Dictionnaire onomastique des chartes du pays et comté de Hainaut, de l'année 1619. No pl. 1782. calf. 4.—

900 **Sala S.J., J. de**, Comment. in secundam secundae D. Thomae de contractibus S. tract.. V. de emptione et venditione, de usuris, etc. Lugd. 1617. 4to. 4.50

901 **Salgado de Somoza, F.**, De regia protectione. Lugd. 1759. fol. Hfvellum. 3.50

902 — De supplicatione. Lugd. 1664. fol. vellum. 4.—

903 **Sallé**, L'esprit des ordonnances et des principaux édits et déclarations de Louis XV, en matière civile, criminelle et bénéficiale. Nouv. éd. Paris, 1771. 4to. calf. 6.—

904 **Salvaing, D. de**, De l'usage des fiefs et autres droits seigneuraux. 2e éd. Grenoble, 1668. fol. calf. 18.—

905 **(Salmasius, Cl.)**, Disquisitio de mutuo. — **C. A. Fabroti**, Epistola de mutuo. C. respons. Cl. Salmasii ad Aeg. Menagium. — **J. J. Vissembachius**, Confutatio diatribae de mutuo. — L. B., J. Maire, 1645. 3 vols. in 1. sm. 8vo. vellum. 3.50

906 **Samhaber, Fr.**, Zur Lehre von der Correalobligation im Röm. und heut. Recht. Erlangen, 1861. boards. 1.25

907 **Saminiatus, J. B.**, Controversiae forenses. Genuae, 1686, et Lucae, 1702. 2 vols. fol. vellum (back damaged). 7.50

908 — — The same. Col. Allobr. 1688. fol. calf. 5.—

909 **Sammlung** auserlesener Landesgesetze welche das Policey- und Cameralwesen zum Gegenstande haben. Hrsg. von J. Beckmann. Frankfurt, 1783–93. 10 vols. in 5. W. pl. 4to. Hfcalf. 75.—
This work forms a continuation to: J. H. L. Berg, Sammlung auserlesener teutschen Landesgesetze, 1780.

910 **Sammlung** des baierischen Bergrechts, mit einer Einleitung in die baierische Bergrechtsgeschichte, von J. G. Lori. München, 1764. fol. Hfcalf. 35.—

911 **Sammlung** altwürttembergischer Statutar-Rechte. Hrsg. von A. L. Reyscher. Tüb. 1834. boards. 7.50

912 **Sanchez S.J., Th.**, De sancto matrimonii sacramento disputationes. Viterbo, 1737. 3 vols. in 1. fol. vellum. (Binding slightly damaged). 18.—

913 **Saur, A.,** Güldiner Auszug und Flusz von Erbschaften dero Erbaigen unnd Lehen-Güter wie die.... ohne Testament vererbt werden. Franckf., N. Bassee, 1580. W. woodcuts in the text. limp vellum. fol. 35.—

914 **Savelli, M. A.,** Practica universale, estratta dalle principali leggi, etc. di Toscana. Firenze, 1681. fol. vellum. 5.—

915 **Savigny, F. C. von,** Geschichte des Röm. Rechts im Mittelalter. 2e Ausg. Heidelb. 1834–51. 7 vols. Hfcalf. (Bindings rubbed). 125.—
From the library of Prof. Eichhorn.

916 — System des heut. Röm. Rechts m. Reg. Berlin, 1840–51. 9 vols. Hfcloth. 30.—

917 — Das Recht des Besitzes. 6e Aufl. Giessen, 1837. Hfcalf. 2.50

918 — Das Obligationenrecht als Theil des heutigen Römischen Rechts. Berlin, 1851, 53. 2 vols. boards. 5.—

919 — Le droit des obligations. Trad. de l'allemand p. C. Gerardin et P. Jozon. Paris, 1863. 2 vols. in 1. 3.—

920 — Vermischte Schriften. Berlin, 1850. 5 vols. boards. 12.—

922 **Scaccia, S.,** De iudiciis causarum civilium, criminalium et haeretecalium. Francof. et Lps. 1669. 2 vols. in 1. fol. vellum. 5.—

923 — De appellationibus. Cum addit. N. Galiardi et decision. coll. J. Renzolio. Ven. 1642. 2 vols. in 1. fol. vellum. (Binding damaged). 4.—

924 — De sententia et re iudicata. Ven. 1669. fol. Hfcalf. 4.50

925 **Scala, P.,** De Consilio Sapientis in forensibus causis adhibendo. ll. IIII. Ven., Aldus, 1560. 4to. old red morocco. 9.—

926 **Scanarolus, J. B.,** De visitatione carceratorum. Romae, 1675. fol. vellum. (back damaged). 5.—

927 **Scarfantonus, J. J.,** Animadvers. ad lucubrationes canonicales Francisci Ceccoperii. Cum decis. S. rotae Romanae. Lucae, 1782. fol. Hfvellum. 3.—

928 **Schaeff, W.,** De jure limitum. Harderovici, J. Moojen, 1739. — **A. A. de Ramdohr,** Commentatio de limitum praescriptione. C. praef. G. H. Ayrerus. Gott. 1746. — 2 pieces. 4to. 4.50

929 **Schaeffner, W.,** Geschichte der Rechtsverfassung Frankreichs. Frankf. 1845–50. 4 vols. Hfcalf. 7.50

930 **Schannat, J. F.,** Sammlung alter histor. Schriften u.s.w., (1361–1499), aus unterschiedl. Archiven. I. Wobey das allgem. Land-Recht wie.... in Teutschland gebräuchlich gewesen. Frankf. 1727. 4to. boards. 2.50

931 **Scheltbriefe** und Schandbilder, ein Rechtsbehelf a. d. 15. und 16. Jahrhundert. Gesammelt und erläut. von O. Hupp. München, 1930. W. 32 reprod. of satyrical drawings. square 4to. boards. 6.—

932 **Schettinus, J.,** De iure offerendi creditori. Acc. enodat. ad ornatum l. 3 Cod. de novationibus. — **Id.,** De tertio veniente ad causam. — etc. Ven. 1702. 3 vols. in 1. fol. vellum. 4.50

933 **Scheurl, C. G. A. v.,** Beitr. z. Bearbeit. des röm. Rechts. Erl. 1853, 54. 2 vols. Hfcalf. 2.50

934 **Schilter, J.,** De Imperii comitum praerogativa ac jure inter ipsos et ordinem equestrem imperii. Argent. 1702. 4to. 2.—

935 — Ad Struvii Syntagma juris feudalis notae. Argent. 1704. — **Idem,** De paragio et apanagio, etc. Argent. 1701. — In 1 vol. 4to. vellum. 3.50

936 **Schlesinger, R.,** Zur Lehre v. d. Formalcontracten und der Querela non numeratae pecuniae. Lpz. 1858. Hfcalf. 2.—

937 **Schliessung, Von vorsichtiger,** der Contracten, oder von denen Cautelen welche ein jeweder in Handel in acht zu nehmen hat, wann er einen Contract sicher schliessen will. Hrsg. von L. v. J. K. J. Hamburg, 1692. 4to. calf. 7.50

938 **Schmidt, K. A.,** Das Interdikten-verfahren der Römer, in geschichtl. Entwickelung. Lpz. 1853. 1.—

939 **Schnaubert, A. J.,** Erläuterung des in Deutschland üblichen Lehnrecht in einem Kommentar über die Böhmerschen principa juris feudalis. Giessen, 1784, 86. 2 vols. 4to. boards. 4.50

940 **Schoene, G.,** Die Amtsgewalt der Fränkischen maiores domus. Brschw. 1856. 1.50

941 **Schöffenspruchsammlung, Leipziger,** (v. 1475–1520). Hrsg. von G. Kisch. Lpz. 1919. bound. 12.50
Quellen z. Geschichte der Rezeption. I.

942 **Schöpffer, T.,** Gerontologia s. tractatus de jure senum. Quedlinb. 1705. 4to. vellum. 3.50

943 **Schott, A. F.,** Sammlungen zu den deutschen Land- und Stadtrechten. Lpz. 1772–75. 3 vols. in 1. 4to. Hfcalf. 10.—

944 **Schottel, J. G.,** De singularibus quibusdam et antiquis in Germania juribus. Kurtzer Tractat von unterschiedlichen Rechten in Teutschland als: Hagestoltzen Recht, Mann Recht, Stadtrecht, Strandrecht, Havereyrecht, Assorantz-Recht, Seerecht, Stapelrecht Vehmrecht, u.s.w. Franckf. 1671. sm. 8vo. vellum. 7.50

945 — — The same. Franckf. 1718. 2 vols. in 1. sm. 8vo. calf. 5.—

946 **Schrader, L.,** Tractatus feudalis. Francof. 1594. 2 vols. in 1. folio. vellum. (Binding damaged). 10.—

947 **Schulenburg, M. de,** De privilegiis et praerogativis nobilium mediatorum in Germania. Francof. 1749. 4to. Hfvellum. 7.50

With fine ex-libris of Koenig de Koenigsthal.

948 **Schulze, C. F.,** Von den Volksversammlungen der Römer. Gotha, 1815. 1.—

949 Des **Schwabenspiegels** Landrechtsbuch. Mit einem Wörterbuche hrsg. von H. G. Gengler. 2e Aufl. Erl. 1875. sm. 8vo. bound. 3.50

950 **Schweppe, A.,** Das römische Privatrecht in seiner heut. Anwendung. 4e Ausg. Gött. 1828–33. 5 vols. boards. 2.75

951 — Römische Rechtsgeschichte und Rechtsalterhümer. 3e Aufl. hrsg. von C. A. Grundler. Gött. 1832. Hfcalf. 1.50

952 **Schwarz, Chr. G.,** Erläuter. des academ. Problematis von des H. R. Reichs Erz- Schild-Herrn-Amt. Altdorff, 1739. W. 3 pl. 4to. boards. 2.—

953 **Schweder, G.,** Introductio in jus publicum imperii Romano-Germanici novissimum. Tubingae, 1685. vellum. 1070 pp. 4.50

954 **Schwerin, C. von,** Einführung in das Studium der germanischen Rechtsgeschichte und ihrer Teilgebiete. Freib. 1922. 1.50

955 **Scoppa, N. V.,** Observat. ad decisiones St. Gratiani. Neap. 1676. W. portrait on front. fol. vellum. 5.—

956 — — The same. Genevae, 1691. fol. Hfvellum. 4.—

957 — Explanationes ad Codicem Fabrianum. Neap. 1702. fol. Hfvellum. 4.—

958 **Selden, J.,** Historical and political discourse of the laws and government of England. London, 1689. fol. calf. 15.—

959 **Sell, C.,** Die Recuperatio der Römer. Brschw. 1887. Hfcalf. 1.25

960 **Senckenberg, H. C.,** Von der kays. höchsten Gerichtsbarkeit in Deutschland. Franckf. 1760. W. 3 pl. 4to. Hfvellum. 4.50

961 **Sentences** civiles du Chatelet de Paris (1395–1505). Publ. p. O. Martin. Paris, 1914. *Reprint.* 1.25

962 **Sententiae** lat. reddit. à Ludov. XIII, Galliar. rege et Navarrae. Paris, 1610. 4to. 2.50

963 **Serres, C.,** Les institutions du droit français suivant l'ordre de celles de Justinien accommodées à la jurisprudence moderne. 2e éd. Paris, 1760. 4to. calf. 6.—

964 — Explication de l'ordonnance de Louis XV.... conc. les donations. Avignon, 1766. sm. 8vo. calf. 2.—

965 **Seta, J. B. A.,** De officio locum tenentis. Ed. 2a. Lucae, 1717. fol. vellum. 5.—

966 **Severus, F. I.,** Ducenturia prima promptuarii, selectorum casuum juridico-practicorum .... d.i.: der ausgerüsteten Schatz-Cammer erstes zweyhundert allerhand auserlesener Gerichts-Fälle. Nürnberg, 1707. W. front. stout vol. 4to. vellum. 6.—

967 **Seydel, M.,** Die Lehre vom Macedon. Senatsbeschlusse. Würzb. 1869. boards. 1.25

968 **Sidney, A.,** Discourses concerning government. London, 1798. fol. calf. 18.—

969 **Sietze, K. F. F.,** Grundbegriff preussischer Staats- und Rechts-Geschichte. Berlin, 1829. boards. 9.—

970 **Sigonius, C.,** De antiquo iure populi Romani. Bon. 1574. fol. vellum. 5.—

971 — — The same. Lps. 1715. 2 vols. sm. 8vo. vellum. 3.50

972 **Smits, N.,** Mosaicarum et Romanarum legum collatio. Haarlem, 1934. 3.90

The text of the „Collatio" is in latin, commentary, etc. in dutch.

973 **Solis, F. de,** Comment. de censibus ll. IV. Mediol. 1614. 4to. vellum. 3.50

974 **Sorge, J.,** Enucleationes casuum forensium s. addit. ad „Jurisprudentiae forenses" ll. X et index. Neap. 1756–58. 11 vols. fol. vellum. 35.—

I–IV. De contractibus inter vivos. — V. De feudis. — VI, VII. De ultimis voluntatibus. — VIII–X. Praxis civilis, criminalis, ecclesiast. — XI. Index.

975 **Sostmann, J. C.,** Jus summi imperantis circa acta decessoris. Ultr. 1699. sm. 8vo. calf. 2.50

976 **Spada, J. B.,** Consilia. Cum annot. et declarat. L. J. Cressini. Parmae, 1720. 3 vols. W. portrait. fol. vellum. (back of vol. 3 damaged). 10.—
977 **Spadazza, C.,** Theatrum viduile s. de viduis ac privilegiis viduilibus. Ferrariae, 1672. fol. vellum. 5.—
978 **Spaltenstein, M.,** Das specif. jurist. Geschäft im röm. Obligationenrecht. Strassb. 1876. 1.—
979 **Span, S.,** Speculum juris metallici, oder: Berg-Rechts-Spiegel, darinnen zu finden was jedweder dem Bergwesen zugethaner, hohen, mittlern und niedern Person.... Befugnisz ist. Dresden, 1698. fol. Hfcalf. 22.—
980 **Spangenberg, E.,** Beyträge zu den teutschen Rechten des Mittelalters, zur Kunde und Kritik der altgerman. Rechtsbücher und des Sachsen- und Schwaben-Spiegels. Halle, 1822. W. 13 pl. 4to. boards. 4.—
981 **Staats-Veränderungen** von Tretucheschei und andern Epauroischen Staaten, durch einen reisenden Persianer Izouf in einiger Briefen an seinen Bruder Machmud. No pl. 1761. Hfcalf. 4.—
982 **Stadarhølsbøk.** The ancient lawbooks Gragas and Jarnsida. Ms. No. 334. fol. in The Arna-Magnaean Collection in the University Library of Copenhagen. W. introd. by O. Larusson. Copenhagen, 1936. W. 216 pl. of facsimile. fol. Hfvellum. 90.—
Corpus codicum Islandicorum medii aevi. Ed. by E. Muncksgaard. Vol. IX.
983 **Stadtrecht, Das,** von München nach bisher ungedruckten Hss. Hrsg. von F. Auer. München, 1840. bound. 12.—
Scarce.
984 **Stahl, F. J.,** Das ältere römische Klagenrecht. 1827. — De matrimonio ob errorem rescindendo comment. 1841. 4to. — Tog. 2 pieces. 1.25
985 **Staibanus, J. B.,** De interesse contractuum et ultimarum voluntatum. Neap. 1654. fol. vellum. (back damaged). 5.—
986 **Stockman, P.,** Opera omnia. Brux. 1686. 4to. calf. 5.—
987 **Stoesser, I. L.,** De auspicio regum. Halae Ven. 1736. 4to. 2.—
988 **Streng, F. W.,** Variae conscriptae consultationes, informationes, relationes et decisiones. Allerley zweiffelhaffter Fälle. Franckf. 1711. 4to. calf. 5.—
989 **Strobl, J.,** Berthold von Regensburg und der Schwabenspiegel. Wien, 1878. (Akad.) 1.—
990 **Strube, D. G.,** Commentatio de jure villicorum vulgo von Meyer-Recht. Ed. 2a adjecta est observationum juris et historiae Germanicae decas. Hildesiae, 1735. 2 parts. — **Id.,** Accessionum ad commentationum de jure villicorum, pars I cui subjungitur tractatio de bonis meierdingicis. Brunsvigae, 1739. — In 1 vol. 4to. Hfvellum. 6.—
991 — Tractatio de statuum provincialium origine et praecipius juribus. Von Landständen. No pl. 1740. — **Lang, K. H.,** Histor. Prüfung des vermeinlichen Alters der teutschen Landstände. Gött. 1796. — **Krüger, F.,** De veterum in Germania provincialium ordinum origine atque natura. Gott. 1843. — In 1 vol. 4to. vellum. 3.50
992 **Struvius, G. A.,** Syntagma jurisprudentiae. Jenae, 1692. 2 vols. in 1. W. engraved titlepage and portrait. 4to. vellum. 5.—
993 **Stryckius, S.,** Operum praestantiorum collectio nova. Halae, 1746–47. 4 vols. in 2. — **Stryckius, S.** et **J. S.,** Opera omnia. Lips, etc. 1744–55. 16 vols. With „Repertorium" by Rhetius. 17 vols. in 9. — Tog. 11 vols. folio. stamped pigskin, with clasps. 75.—
Complete set.
994 — De cautelis testamentorum. Ed. 2a. Halae, 1708. W. portrait. 4to. vellum. 3.—
995 — Succinctae annot. ad W. A. Lauterbachii Compendium Digest. 6a ed. Lps. 1712. W. portrait. 4to. vellum. 2.50
996 **Summenhart, C.,** De contractibus licitis atque illicitis. In quo de mutuatione, obligatione, usura, etc. Ven., F. Zilettus, 1580. fol. Hfvellum. (Titlepage with some wormholes). 8.—
997 **Summermann, J. H.,** Conjecturae de origine et progressu testament. apud Romanos ac Germanos aliosque populos. Berol. 1735. 4to. calf. 2.50
998 **Surdus, J. P.,** De alimentis. Genevae, 1645. fol. boards. 5.—
999 — Consilia. Ven. et Aug. Taurin. 1584–1610. 4 vols. fol. vellum. (Binding of vol. I is broken). 25.—
1000 — Decisiones. Lugd. 1607. 2 vols. in 1. fol. vellum. (back damaged). 5.—
1001 — — The same. Francof. 1664. fol. vellum. 5.—
1002 **Syring, C. H.,** Aurea praxis juris decimandi, oder das Zehend-Recht und dessen heutiger Gebrauch in und ausserhalb Teutschland. Augsburg, 1735. W. front. 4to. vellum. 5.—

1003 **Taidinge, Die Salzburgischen.** Hrsg. von H. Siegel und K. Tomaschek. Wien, 1870. bound. (Oesterreich. Weisthümer, Bd. I). 5.—

1004 **Tasson, J. D.,** Observat. iurisdict. ad regiam pragmaticam sanctionem editam 1617, quae dicitur de antefato. Neap. 1716. fol. Hfvellum. 3.75

1005 **Thanner, J. A.,** De captivis in bello, vulgo von Kriegs-Gefangenen. Argentor. 1714. 4to. 6.—

1006 **Theodosiani** codicis ll. V priores. Rec. W. F. Clossius et A. Peyton. Instr. C. F. Ch. Wenck. Lps. 1825. boards. 1.—

1007 **Theodosii jun.** et Valentiniani III novellae leges. Ex Ottobanio ms. codice ed. A. Zirardinus. Faventia, 1766. W. facs. Hfcalf. 2.50

1008 **Thévenot d'Essaule de Savigny,** Traité des substitutions fidéicommissaires, cont. toutes les connoissances essentielles selon le droit romain et le droit français. Av. des notes sur l'ordonnance de 1747. Paris, 1778. 4to. calf. 15.—

1009 **Thibault, F. T.,** Histoire des loix et usages de la Lorraine et du Barrois dans les matières bénéficiales. Nancy, 1763. fol. calf. 20.—

1010 **Thore, I. B. de,** Vota decisiva civilia, criminalia, etc. Neap. 1655. 2 vols. fol. vellum. 7.—

1011 **Thucelius, C.,** Electa jurispublici curiosa, vorstellend das alte Fürsten-Recht, samt den Novem-Vitatum vornehmlich aber der fürstlichen Hauszes Wurtemberg Jura wegen des Reichs-Bannerer- und Fendrich-Ambts. Franckf. 1694. 4to. vellum. 6.—

1012 **Thudichum, F.,** Die Gau- und Markverfassung in Deutschland. Giessen, 1860. boards. 7.50

1013 **Tigerström, F. G. de,** De judicibus apud Romanos. Berol. 1826. 1.25

1014 **Tiraquellus, A.,** De utroque retractu municipali et conventionali. Ed. 4a. Lugd., G. Rovillius, 1584. fol. Hfvellum. 10.—

1015 — — The same. Ed. 3a. Lugduni, G. Rovillius, 1554. — **Id.,** Tractatus, cessante causa cessat effectus. Le mort saisit le vif. De jure constituto possessorii L. Boves hoc sermone, de verborum significatione. Ed. 3a. Lugduni, G. Rovillius, 1559. — 2 vols. in 1. folio. oaken boards, back pigskin. 50.—

Both titles in a fine woodcut border and both with the portrait of Tiraquellus on the verso of the titlepage.

1016 **Tomasinus, J. P.,** De donariis ac tabellis votivis. 2a ed. auct. Patavii, 1645. W. 1 pl. and ill. 4to. vellum. 4.—

1017 **Tomasius, B.,** Decas tractatus continens infrascriptos personarum statum nec non ultim. volunt. Ven. 1629. fol. vellum. (Binding broken.) 3.50

1018 **Tondutus, P. F. de,** De praeventione iudiciale. Col. Allobr. 1653. 2 vols. in 1. fol. vellum. 3.50

1019 — — The same. Lugd. 1673. fol. vellum. 4.—

1020 — De pensionibus ecclesiasticis. Lugd. 1662. 2 vols. in 1. W. portrait. fol. vellum. 4.—

1021 — — The same. Ed. 2a. Lugd. 1671. fol. vellum. 4.—

1022 — Quaest. et resolut. legales, beneficiales et controversiae civiles. Lugd. 1683. 2 vols. fol. vellum. 7.50

1023 **Tornovius, P.,** De feudis Mecklenburgicis eorumque jure. Güstrov, 1708, 11. 2 vols. in 1. W. 2 portr. 4to. vellum. 12.50

1024 **Tractatus varii** de inventarii beneficio ac eius conficiendi forma, author. A. de Ubaldus, G. Papa, M. Grassus, e.a. Aug. Taurin. 1612. fol. vellum. (Binding damaged). 5.—

1025 **Tractatus** de dote. Autores: Baldus Novellus, Campezius, Odofredus, Gotomanus etc. Venet., M. Rubinus, 1571. fol. vellum. (Binding broken). 9.—

1026 **Tractatus** juridicus de jure canum, oder Hunds-Recht..... beygefügt das Recht der Tauben und Hüner. Franckfurt, 1719. 4to. 6.—

1027 **Tractatus** juridici III. de subhastationibus.... von verschiedenen und vornehmsten Arten derer Vergantungen oder Gant Recht, nemlich. I M. Pegii, Tractat von Vergantungen. II J. O. Taboris, idem, III A. Schoene, idem. Franckf. 1731. W. front. 4to. vellum. 6.—

1028 **Tractatus** auctorum (A. Faber, C. A. Blancardus, F. Solsona, e.a.) qui hactenus de laudimiis commentarios conscripserunt. F. Solsona rest. Aug. Taurin. 1629. fol. vellum. (Binding broken). 4.50

1029 **Tranchedinus, F. A.,** Consultationes variae. Mediol. 1681 et Ticin. Reg. 1691. 2 vols. fol. vellum. 7.50

1030 **Trentacinquius, A.,** De substitutionibus. Ven., D. Zenarius, 1588. fol. vellum. 6.50

1031 — Variae resolutiones. Ven. 1609. 3 vols. in 1. fol. vellum. 7.—

1032 **(Trützschler, F. K. A. v.),** Anweisung zur Abfassung rechtlicher Aufsätze über Handlungen der willkürlichen Gerichtsbarkeit. Lpz. 1783, 84. 2 vols. calf. 4.50
1033 **Tulden, D.,** [Opera juridica]. Lovan. 1702–12. 4 vols. in 5. fol. calf. 35.—
I. In IV ll. Institutionum commentarius. — II–III. Comment. in Digesta. — IV. Comment. ad Codicem Justin. — V. De civili regimine.
1034 — De civili regimine. Lovan. 1702. fol. calf. 5.—
1035 **Turrecremata, J. à,** In Gratiam decretorum primam commentarii. In tractatum de poenitentia commentarii. In tractatum de consecratione commentari. Nic. Boerij. Burdegalensis praesidis additionibus, et summariis illustrat. Lugduni, Blasius Guido, 1555. 3 parts in 2 vols. folio. oaken boards, back pressed pigskin. (A small hole in the last leaf of the index). 30.—
1036 **Turricellius, J. B.,** De rebus ecclesiae non alienandis. — **Id.,** De benefitiorum unione. — Ferrariae, 1674. 2 vols. in 1. fol. vellum. 5.—
1037 **Ubaldini, U.,** Pratica de notari o sia formolario d'instrumenti. Ed. 2a expurg. et illustr. a. D. Ubaldini. Neap. 1714. fol. vellum. 3.50
1038 **Urceolus, J.,** De transactionibus cum decis, s. rotae Rom. Bon. 1679. fol. vellum. 3.—
1039 — — The same. Col. Allobr. 1685. fol. vellum. 4.—
1040 — — The same. Genevae. 1686. fol. vellum. 4.—
1041 — — The same. Ed. 3a. Lugd. 1688. fol. vellum. 4.50
1042 — Consultationes forenses. Ed. 3a. Col. Allobr. 1686. 2 vols. in 1. fol. 4.50
1043 — Decisiones inclytae rotae Florentinae cont. materias contractuum, ultimarum voluntatum. etc. Flor. 1692. fol. calf. 5.—
1044 — — The same. Flor. 1693. fol. vellum. 5.—
1045 **Urkunden, Ausgewählte,** zur ausserdeutschen Verfassungsgeschichte seit 1776. Hrsg. von W. Altman. Berlin, 1897. bound. 3.—
Interleaved, with annotations by Prof. Bussemaker.
1046 **Ursaya a Bosco, D.,** Institutiones criminales usui etiam forensi. Romae, 1706. fol. calf. (back damaged, waterstained). 3.—
1047 **Valentibus, F. de,** Dissertat. fiscales. Romae, 1751. 3 vols. fol. vellum. 10.—
1048 **Valin, R. J.,** Nouveau commentaire sur l'ordonnance de la marine, du mois d'août 1681. La Rochelle, 1760. 2 vols. 4to. calf. 20.—
1049 **Vandenpeereboom, A.,** Le Conseil de Flandre à Ypres, 1451–1498. Préc. de: Des cours de justice qui ont exercé juridiction souveraine sur la ville d'Ypres et la West-Flandre. Ypres, 1872–74. 3 vols. in 1. W. pl. 2. Hfcalf. 12.—
1050 **Vanderanus, P.,** De privilegiis creditorum. Antv., J. Bellerus, 1560. sm. 8vo. vellum. 6.—
1051 **Vantius, S.,** Tractatus de multitatibus processuum ac sententiarum, causarum patronis, caeterisque legum studiosis, etc. Venetiis, F. Bindonus, 1556. sm. 8vo. vellum cover. 6.—
1052 **Vasquinus Pincianus, P.,** De successionum creatione, progressu et resolutione. Ven., H. Scotus, 1573. fol. limp vellum. 7.50
1053 **Véla de Orena, J.,** Dissertat. iuris controversi. Lugd. 1675. 2 vols. in 1. fol. vellum. (back damaged). 4.75
1054 **(Ventura, C.),** Trésor politique, contenant les relations, instructions et traités appartenants à l'intelligence de la raison d'Etat. Trad. de l'Italien par N. du Fossé. Paris, 1611. 3 vols. in 1. 4to. vellum. 5.—
1055 **Verde, F.,** Tyrocinium ac universi iuris civilis instructio. Ven. 1711. 2 vols. in 1. fol. vellum. 4.—
1056 — — The same. Ed. 3a. Neap. 1728. 2 vols. in 1. fol. vellum. 5.—
1057 **Verloo, J. C.,** Codex Brabanticus, seu corpus juris edictalis Brabantiae et Limburgiae. Brux. (1781). fol. Hfcalf. 7.50
1058 **Verzeichniss** der Rheinischen Weistümer. Vorarbeit zu der unternommenen Ausgabe. Trier, 1883. W. map. 2.50
1059 **Vespignanus, J. S.,** De emptione, et venditione nec non de expensis, quae fiunt in causis civilibus. Imolae, 1702. fol. vellum. (Back damaged). 4.50
1060 **Vidaillan, de,** Histoire des conseils du roi depuis l'origine de la monarchie jusqu'à nos jours. Paris, 1856. 2 vols. in 1. Hfcalf. 12.—
1061 **Vilaplana, A. de,** Illustrationes feudales et emphyteuticales. — **Id.,** De brachio militari et pristina nobilitate Gotholanorum. — Barcin. 1687, 82. 2 vols. in 1. fol. Hf-vellum. 6.—
1062 **Vinnius, A.,** Jurisprudentiae contractae s. partitionum juris civilis ll. IV. Rott., J. Naeranus, 1663. W. front. 4to. vellum. 5.—

1063 **Vinogradoff, P.,** Outlines of historical jurisprudence. Oxford, 1920, 22. 2 vols. cloth. 12.50
I. Introduction. Tribal law. — II. The jurisprudence of the Greek city.

1064 — Collected papers. W. Memoir by H. A. L. Fisher. Oxford, 1928. 2 vols. W. portrait. cloth. 12.—
I. Historical (the text of Bractow. — Transfer of land in old english law. — Das Buchland. — The work of Rome. — A history of local government. — etc.) — II. Jurisprudence (Aristotle on legal redress. — Greek law. — Ludwig Mitteis. — Histor. types of internat. law. — Quelques problèmes d'histoire du droit angl-normand. — etc.).

1065 **Vitriarius, Ph. R.,** Institutiones juris publici Romano-Germanici. Ed. nova. Acc. Aurea Bulla, Instrumenta Pacis Westphalicae, etc. L. B., T. Haak et S. Luchtmans, 1730. 2 vols. in 1. Hfcalf. 4.50

1066 **Vizzanius, C. E.,** De mandatis principum, seu de officio eorum, qui in provincias cum imperio mittuntur. Amst., J. Blaeu, 1658. 4to. vellum. 6.—

1067 **(Voltaire),** Histoire du parlement de Paris, par Mr. l'abbé Big.... Amst. (Paris) 1770. 2 vols. calf. 10.—
Original edition.

1068 **Vrind, G.,** De Cassii Dionis vocabulis quae ad ius publicum pertinent. Hag. Com., 1923. 2.50

1069 **Wachsmuth, C. U.,** Versuch einer systemat. Darstellung der Patrimobial-Gerichtsverfassung der Rittergüther nach gemeinen und sächsischen Rechten. Lpz. 1808. boards. 2.50

1070 **Walter, F.,** Geschichte des röm. Rechts bis auf Justinian. 2e Aufl. Bonn, 1845. 2 vols. boards. 2.50

1071 **Walter, P.,** L'ancienne administration de la principauté de Montbéliard. Montbél. 1907. 4.—

1072 **Warnkoenig, L. A.,** und **L. Stein,** Französische Staats- und Rechtsgeschichte. 2e Ausg. Basel, 1875. 3 vols. Hfcalf. 28.—

1073 **Weber, A.,** Der Centenar nach der Karolingischen Kapitularien. Lpz. 1894. 1.—

1074 **Weise, C.,** De lectione novellarum.... nec non genealogia comitum Leiningensium, quam exhib. Rittershusius. Lps. 1696. 2.50

1075 **Weisthümer, Die Tirolischen.** Hrsg. von I. v. Zingerle u. K. Th. von Inama-Sternegg. Wien, 1875–91. 4 vols. in 5. bound. (Oesterreich. Weisthümer, Bd. II–V). 40.—

1076 **Weixer, J. C.,** De jure dominorum et subditorum. Von Recht und Gerechtigkeit der Grundherrn und Unterthanen. Uber den 21. Titul der Chur-Bayrischen Landrecht. München, 1718. 4to. vellum. 5.—

1077 **Werndle, J. von,** Tractat vom Zehend-Recht. Wie solches in dem gantzen Röm. Reich im Gebrauch ist. Samt Anhang welcher die Zehend-Ordnungen, u.s.w. in sich begreiffet. Verm. hrsg. von C. Loelio. Nürnberg, 1722. W. front. 4to. vellum. 6.—

1078 **Wernher, J. B. à,** Selectae observationes forenses. Jenae, 1749–1756. 3 vols. fol. calf. (Binding damaged). 10.—

1079 **Wernz S. J., F. X.,** Jus decretalium. T. I. Introductio in jus decretalium. Ed. 3a. Prati, 1913. 2.50
All published.

1080 **Wiardi, W.,** De aleatoribus. (Cod. Rom. III. 43. 2). Lugd. Bat. 1731. 4to. 1.50

1081 **Wieling, A.,** De jure Sanctionis pragmaticae, divi Caroli VI. Ultr. 1741. 4to. 1.50

1082 **Wigand, P.,** Die Provinzialrechte der Fürstenthümer Paderborn und Corvey in Westphalen nebst ihrer rechtsgeschichtl. Entwickelung. Lpz. 1832. 3 vols. boards. 12.—

1083 — Die Provinzialrechte des Fürstenthums Minden, der Graffschaften Ravensberg und Rietberg, der Herrschaft Rheda un des Amtes Reckenberg in Westphalen, nebst ihrer rechtsgeschichtl. Entwickelung und Begründung. Lpz. 1834. 2 vols. boards. 12.—

1084 **Wilda, W. E.,** Das Strafrecht der Germanen. Halle, 1842. boards. *Scarce.* 45.—
Geschichte des Deutschen Strafrechts. I.

1085 **(Wilde, J.),** Sueciae historia pragmatica, quae vulgo jus publicum dicitur. Holmiae, 1731. 4to. vellum. (Librarystamp on titlepage). 6.—

1086 **Winterfeld, C. M. D. von,** Abhandlung über das Retractrecht der Söhne und Minorennen auf altväterliche Stammlehne besonders in Mecklenburg. M. Anlagen. Gött. 1803. 3.—

1087 **Woldenberg, C.,** De numeris utriusque iuris et canonici et civilis. Francof. 1670. W. portrait. 4to. 3.50

1088 **(Wynne, E.),** Eunomus or dialogues conc. the law and constitution of England. London, 1774. 4 vols. calf. 4.50

1089 **Xammar, J. P.,** Res judicatae in sacro regio senatu Cathaloniae sub diversis definitionibus c. rationalibus s (si mavis) allegationibus. Barcinon. 1657. fol. vellum. (Waterstained). 9.—

1090 **Yanguas y Miranda, J.,** Diccionarios de los fueros del reino de Navarra a y de les leyes vigentes promulgadas hasta las cortes de 1817 y 18 incl. San Sebastian, 1828, 29. With Adiciones. 2 vols. in 1. calf. 20.—

1091 **Zacchias, L.,** De salarii seu operariorum mercede. Romae, 1679. fol. vellum. 5.—

1092 **Zacchias, P.,** Quaestiones medico-legales. C. Decisiones s. rotae Romanae. Lugd. 1661. 2 vols. fol. vellum. 9.—

1093 **Zacchias, S.,** De obligatione camerali. Romae, 1647. fol. Hfvellum. 7.50

1094 **Zachariä, K. S.,** Sulla als Ordner des röm. Freystaates. Heidelb. 1834. 2 vols. boards. 1.25

1095 **Zahn, B. C.,** Tractatus de mendaciis ex sacris juridicis, ethicis, etc. Col. Agr. 1686. 4to. vellum. 2.50

1096 — Politia municipalis sive de jure et jurisdictione civitatum municipalium. Ed. Th. E. Zahn. Lippiae, 1713. 4to. vellum. (1500 pp.). 7.50

1097 **Zanchius, C.,** De laesione. Romae, 1771. fol. Hfvellum. 4.—

1098 — — The same. Ed. alt. Romae, 1825. fol. d. vél. 4.—

1099 — De societate. Romae, 1786. fol. Hfvellum. 4.—

1100 — — The same. Flor. 1838. fol. Hfvellum. 3.—

1101 — De praelatione creditorum. Flor. 1839. fol. Hfvellum. 3.50

1102 **Zanchus, H.,** Repetitio famigerati § cum ita l. haeredes mei ff. ad senatus cons. Trebellia. Ven., Damianus Zenarus, 1576. fol. Hfcalf. 6.50

1103 **Zanger, J.,** Tractatus duo: unus de exceptionibus alter de quaestionibus seu torturis reorum. Francof. 1617. 4to. vellum. 10.—

1104 — — The same. Witteberg, 1665. 4to. vellum. 6.—

1105 **Zasius, U.,** Singularia responsa, sive intellectus juris singulares insigni accessione locupletati. Basil., M. Isingrin, 1541. fol. vellum cover (old manuscript). 75.—
Some wormholes.
Bound up with: **Tornielli, H.,** Tractatus, si quod ago, non valet, ut ago, an valeat ut valere potest. Patavii, G. Perchacinus, 1558. — **Id.,** In L. A. Testatore ff. de cond. et demonst. et in l. in quartam ff. ad l. Falcid..... interpretis. Patavii, 1558.

1106 **Zaulis, D. de,** Observationes canonicae, civiles, criminales, etc. Ed. 2a. Romae, 1723. 2 vols. fol. vellum. 6.50

1107 **Zeitschrift für geschichtl. Rechtswissenschaft.** Hrsg. von von Savigny, Eichhorn, Rudorff, u.A. Berlin, 1815–50. 15 vols. boards. 175.—
All published. Very scarce.

1108 **Ziegler, C.,** Rabulistica s. de artibus rabulariis. Dresd., 1685. 4to. boards. 2.25

1109 **Zincken, C. F. W.,** Kurze und deutl. Einleitung zur Kriegs-Rechtsgelahrsamkeit in Deutschland. Magdeburg, 1772. 4to. boards. 2.—

1110 **Zoeller, M.,** Römische Staats- und Rechtsaltertümer. Breslau, 1885. 2.—

1111 **Zuffus, J.,** De criminalis processus legitimatione. Cum desicion. s. rotae Rom. Romae, 1665. fol. vellum. 4.—

SUPPLEMENT

1112 **Aalten Jr., S. J. L. van,** Histor.-critische beschouwing van de leer der trias politica. 's-Grav. 1886. 2.—

1113 **Asverus, G.,** Denunciation der Römer und ihr geschichtlicher Zusammenhang mit dem ersten processeinleitenden Decrete. Lpz. 1843. 1.—

1114 **Cassan, J. de,** La recherche des droicts du roy, et de la couronne de France. Rouen, 1643. sm. 8vo. calf. 5.—

1115 **Cicero,** De legibus, rec. J. Bake. Lugd. Bat. 1842. Hfcalf. 1.50

1116 **Collection** of about 450 jur. theses in latin, publ. at Louvain, 1818–30. Bound in 17 vols. 4to. and 18 vols. 8vo. Hfcalf. 50.—

1117 **Dubois, L.,** Le régime de la brasserie à Lille des origines à la Révolution (1279–1789). Lille, 1912. 6.—

1118 **Frets, F.,** Welke zijn de regten, het aanzien etc. der regtsgeleerden in het Rom. rijk geweest, van af Augustus tot Justinianus? — **Holtius, A. C.,** Ad quaest. quaenam fuere jura, ... dignitas jureconsult. Roman inde a temp. C. Augusti usque ad dec. Justiniani? Amst. 1822. 4to. Hfcalf. (Akad.). 3.50

1119 **Gierke, O.,** Schuld und Haftung im älteren deutschen Recht. Breslau, 1910. (Untersuch. sur dtschen Staats- und Rechtsgesch. Heft. 100). 6.—

1120 **Goguet, A. Y.,** et **A. C. Fugère,** De l'origine des loix, des arts, et des sciences; et de leurs progrès chez les anciens peuples. Paris, 1809. 3 vols. W. pl. Hfcalf. 3.—

1121 **Gonne, I. G.,** De commento Speculi suevici seu alemannici. Erlangae, 1753. 4to. 2.50

1122 **Hartmann, O. E.,** Die röm. Gerichtsverfassung. Gött. 1859. 1.—

1123 **Hevia Bolanos, J. de,** Curia Philipica, donde se trata de los juicios civiles y criminales, eclesiast. y seculares. Nueva impr. Madrid, 1783. folio. vellum. (*Binding damaged*). 9.—

The 2d part contains: de la Mercancia y contratacion de tierra y mar."

1124 **Leyser, A. à,** Meditationes ad Pandectas. Ed. nova et ed. 3a. Indices adj. G. A. Jenichen. Lps. 1761–1786. 13 vols. in 10. 4to. Hfcalf. 40.—

1125 **Machiavel,** Oeuvres. Amst., H. Desbordes, 1697. 6 vols. sm. 8vo. vellum. 15.—

1126 **Savigny, Fr. C. van,** Das Recht des Besitzes. 5e Aufl. Giessen, 1827. 1.50

1127 **Swinderen, P. J. van,** De aera Molacitano et Salpensano. Gron. 1856. 2.—